WALTHAMSTOW
PAST

For SUE, JANE and SHARON
and in memoriam
A.D.L. and W.G.S.T

Acknowledgements

The author would like to thank the staff of Vestry House Museum, especially Kirsty Brody, Josephine Parker and Anna Smith, for their help with source material, particularly for providing access to the watercolour and painting collection.

The Illustrations

The following have kindly given permission to reproduce illustrations:
Butler and Hegarty: *35*
Roger Cline: *2, 3, 5, 8, 9, 11, 14, 20, 23, 33, 39, 40, 44, 47, 49, 51, 59, 70, 73, 79, 106, 113, 114, 120, 136, 138, 146, 150, 151*
London Borough of Hackney Archives: *74, 89*
Science Museum, London: *142*
London Borough of Waltham Forest, Vestry House Museum: *1, 6, 7, 10, 12, 13, 15, 16, 17, 18, 19, 21, 22, 24, 25, 26, 27, 28, 29, 30, 31, 32, 34, 36, 37, 38, 41, 42, 43, 48, 50, 52, 53, 54, 55, 56, 57, 58, 60, 61, 62, 63, 64, 65, 66, 67, 71, 78, 80, 81, 83, 85, 86, 87, 88, 90, 92, 93, 95, 96, 98, 99, 100, 101, 105, 107, 108, 110, 111, 115, 116, 117, 121, 123, 124, 126, 127, 129, 131, 132, 133, 134, 135, 137, 139, 140, 141, 143, 144, 147, 148, 149, 152, 153 and the jacket*
Sir Henry Warner: *68, 69, 94*
David Mander: *4, 46, 76, 77, 82, 91, 104, 112, 122, 130, 154, 155*
Historical Publications: *72, 75, 84, 97, 109, 118, 119, 125, 128, 145*

First published 2001
by Historical Publications Ltd
32 Ellington Street, N7 8PL
(Tel: 020-7607 1628)

ISBN 0 948667 73 7
British Library Cataloguing-in-Publication Data
A catalogue record for this book is available from the British Library

Typeset in Palatino by Historical Publications Ltd
Reproduction by G & J Graphics, London EC2
Printed in Zaragoza, Spain by Edelvives

WALTHAMSTOW PAST

David Mander

HISTORICAL PUBLICATIONS

Between the wood and the water

JOHN COE'S MAP

Standing on a busy main road of a London suburb, and trying not to breathe in too deeply, it is hard to imagine that your surroundings of slow moving traffic, reflected lights from the windows of sundry multiple stores, and the scents of homogenised burger or gas grilled kebab have not always been a part of this particular landscape. Of course there must have been a time when this place was, well less built up, less suburban even. But a village? With fields? And less than five thousand people? Walthamstow?

Let us reverse that rush a moment and go back virtually a hundred and ninety years to a room in the local museum. Now it is the front gallery used for temporary exhibitions, but in 1814 it was the vestry room of the parish workhouse, where the men (no women) who made up Walthamstow's local governing body met to administer parochial affairs. A year before, on 13 August 1813, the vestrymen had discussed the age old problem of collecting local taxes, and had minuted that 'Sundry Houses and Cottages have not been assessed to the Poor Rate.' The meeting directed their clerk to 'take a full account of every House and Cottage within the parish that has been omitted in order that in future the whole may be assessed and pay the Rate accordingly'.

Now, one year on, they could see the results of that instruction. The vestry room had been extended into the workhouse yard some forty years before, and there was plenty of room to spread out the new map of the parish, prepared by their parish clerk. It had been a long labour, but for the first time it gave the parish sight of local houses, fields, and land use, a firm basis for local taxation, and, as some may have also thought, it could also come in handy for buying and selling land.

Each plot of land had its own number and alongside the map was a bound volume, giving details of owners, occupiers, and what the land was used for – meadow, pasture, house and outhouses, pleasure gardens, roads, lanes and paths. The clerk had been thorough and the vestrymen considered their money well spent. The 675 houses identified in the census of the same year, homes to 4,304 people, were shown, and the outline of the more important gentlemen's houses were clearly distinguished. There was the T-shape of ornamental water of Shern Hall and the clover leaf of the more recent lake of Belle Vue House. A sufficiency of drawn trees surrounded the grounds of Jeremiah Harman's park, improved on the recommendations of Humphry Repton some thirty years before. Even the strips of the common fields were shown in dotted outline.

In 1822 the next vestry clerk, John Coe, took the project one stage further. Coe, who came to Walthamstow in 1815, obtained the permission of the vestry to contract a firm of London engravers to produce a printed copy of the map, with some colour shading. No record of the decision of the vestry survives, but it is tempting to think of that precursor of the local council crowding round the long table in the vestry room, after approving the latest report of the workhouse committee, to inspect the newly engraved map, suitably shaded, and with each plot numbered up. Alongside would have been a book of reference, giving owner, occupier, a description of the property and its acreage.

A copy of Coe's map hangs in what is now the panelled room at the back of the Vestry House Museum on the way up to what was once the female paupers' dormitory, but which now houses the archive search room. The original book of reference does not survive, but the map numbers were used in the 1836 rating assessment. So what survives is a layer of three periods, a base of 1814, with some re-drawing to show houses in 1822, and with the owners and occupiers of fourteen years later. But the map that bears John Coe's name still serves as the best introduction to a Walthamstow that was pre-industrial, pastoral, a place of residence for the substantial City man who did not have to be in his office on a daily basis, but also a place of agricultural poverty and localised hardship.

GEOLOGY AND GEOGRAPHY

In the medieval world Walthamstow was a well balanced parish, with a river to the west providing fish and flooded land well suited for grazing, and forest to the east, with pannage for pigs and with the possibility of cutting down the trees to make new fields or 'braches', as the population increased. The land rises steeply to the north east from the River Lea to the mound of Higham Hill,

1. *Section of John Coe's map of 1822.*

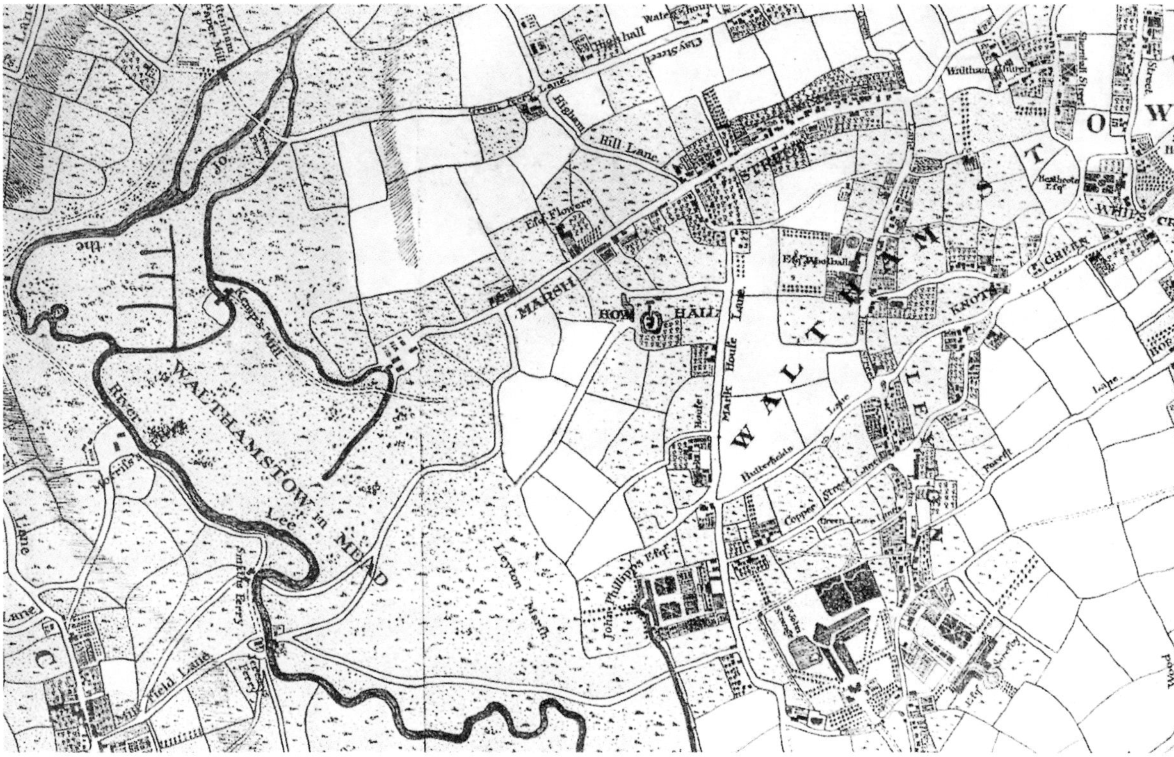

2. *Section of John Rocque's map of 1744, showing the Walthamstow area.*

which is 75 feet high, and there is a further hill midway between the Lea and Epping Forest of 125 feet, on which eminence stands the old parish church of Walthamstow. There are gravel terraces near the Lea, but further east the gravels mix with London clay.

The Lea forms the western boundary of the parish from Chingford to Leyton. The Ching – in the fourteenth century the Bourne – flows south from Chingford Hatch and then westwards by one of the manor houses, Salisbury Hall, to join the Lea at Hangers' Bourne. South of Essex Hall, the Fleet River (not to be confused with the more famous Fleet which runs from Hampstead and Highgate to Blackfriars) diverged from the Lea and runs parallel down past the Ferry Boat Inn and then it provided power for the Coppermill and its various industries before rejoining the Lea at the northern edge of Walthamstow Marshes. There were smaller streams – the Higham Hill brook ran from just south of an ancient farm, Moons at Chapel End round the south side of Higham Hill common field and across Blackhorse Lane to the Dagenham Brook, which in turn ran past Low Hall into Leyton. West of Wood Street was the Sharnall or Filth Stream, which provided the original name for Sharnall Street, later elevated to the modern Shernhall Street, and with its own Shern Hall. Further south this noisome stream became the Phillebrook in Leyton.

THE HAMLETS

An early nineteenth-century antiquarian could still distinguish the hamlets that made up the parish. The northern part that had formed the ancient manor of Higham was still the more sparsely settled. In the north east the settlement at 'The Hale' was mentioned in 1285, known later as Hale End or Woodend and with its nucleus just south of the crossing over the Ching at the junction of Green Lane (later Jack's or Inks Green Lane and now Larkshall Road and Hale End Road) and Hale End Lane (the modern junction of Hale End Road and Wadham Road).

To the west was Chapel End, taking its name from the chantry chapel of St Edward built in the mid fifteenth century, with its centre at the

3. *Hillyer's Bridge over the River Lea in 1836, with the Ferry Boat public house in the background. From a painting by C. Marshall.*

Crooked Billet junction, and with Salisbury Hall manor house lying to the north. Moons Lane, the present Billet Road, ran east to another hamlet round Higham Bensted's manor house (later Essex Hall), Higham Hill. Amber Lane, now Folly Lane, ran north to Chingford Hall, skirting fields now beneath the Banbury Reservoir. In the fifteenth century there had been seven houses here, but five were demolished between the mid sixteenth and the mid eighteenth centuries, an indication that the settlement was in comparative decline.

Further south the early hamlets were round the church and at King's End, later Knotts Green in Leyton. Part of this lay in the Walthamstow Slip, a detached strip of 98 acres whose boundaries ran to the south of the main parish boundary and in parallel with it. The other detached part of Walthamstow, in Wye mead, lying north-east in what is now Chingford, probably arose through the attachment of land to Higham manor in early medieval times, but the origin of the Slip is not known for certain. It is likely to have arisen over a refusal by Leyton parish to bury a dead body found on the land – Walthamstow people are said to have carried out the burial and claimed the strip of land as a consequence. The Slip was not finally merged with Leyton civil parish until 1878, while the detached land in Chingford was re-united with that parish in 1882.

By 1699, the date of the first extant manorial map, the majority of buildings in the southern part of the parish were in Marsh Street (now High Street), at Church End, along Shernhall Street, Clay Street (now that part of Forest Road between Blackhorse Road and Wood Street) and Hoe Street. By 1822 Marsh Street and Wood Street were the most populous, though there were also groups of houses on Shernhall Street near the Church Lane junction and on cleared land to the north east of Whipps Cross.

ROADS

There are three lines of north-south roads, and three running east-west. The main north-south route was from Waltham Holy Cross through Chingford Mount, passing through Chapel End, Greenleaf Lane (now Hoe Street between Forest Road and High Street) and the old Hoe Street to Leyton and Stratford. Hoe (meaning ridge) Street was so named in 1513. To the east lanes ran from Chingford down the side of the Forest to Whipps Cross. The most westerly of the north-south routes saw the least traffic – Folly Lane was a horseway in the early sixteenth century, but was never improved.

The main east-west road ran from Epping to Tottenham and would have been used by those going to Epping market. At the forest side it was Hangerstrete in 1519 (later Hagger Lane), before becoming Clay Street (Priorstrete in 1532, from the Priory of Holy Trinity, Aldgate, whose rectory manor abutted on this part of Forest Road) and then Mill Lane. Ralph de Tony was required to make bridges over the Fleet and Lea rivers in 1277 and a later lady of the manor, the Countess of Rutland, was presented at quarter sessions in 1595 for failing to keep a bridge on the way to Tottenham mill in proper repair. There was a ferry alongside the bridge in 1722, and in 1760 William Maynard rebuilt the bridge with tolls for horses and carriages. The ferry house alongside became the Ferry Boat Inn and Maynard's bridge, or the Ferry Bridge, made of timber with iron abutments, took its alternative name of Hillyer's Turnpike from the ferryman of the time, Sacheverell Hillyer, who was also the landlord of the inn.

The Epping route was improved by the construction of the Woodford New Road some six years after Coe's map, in 1828-30. North of Clay Street, Blackhorse Lane (from the Black House, on the site of the present Clock House, Pretoria Avenue), joined Moons Lane to link Higham Hill to Hale End. A bridge over the Lea at Higham Hill was recorded in 1594, but not later, and in 1687 a ferry, called Boulton's, and by the late nineteenth century Games's, operated until 1897 when the Banbury reservoir was built. Jimmy Games, the ferryman, piloted his boat across the Lea when summoned by a bell.

The third east-west route ran from Wood Street via Wyatt's Lane through Church Hill to Marsh Street. From the bottom of Marsh Street, Water Lane led south across the marshes to Lockbridge in Leyton, where there was also a ford. This was the principal crossing place to Hackney and Clapton, and was supplemented by a wooden causeway, repaired by Walthamstow benefactor George Monoux in the early sixteenth century. This was in ruins by the 1580s. The Lock bridge finally collapsed at some date between 1612 and 1630, after which a ferry operated, known by the eighteenth century as Jeremy's ferry. The ford was still called Lockbridge in 1646, but a bridge crossing was not reinstated until the Lea Bridge Turnpike Act of 1757 restored the former road route by Hemstall Green and Blackbridge in Leyton and extinguished Jeremy's ferry. A less important ferry to the north, linking High Hill in Hackney to a footpath across Walthamstow marshes was known as Morris's in 1742. This ferry survived until 1947 and may have been of considerable antiquity for an Anglo-Saxon log boat dating back to AD *c*.950 was discovered in 1987 near here on the Hackney side of the river at Big Hill.

EARLY HISTORY

Walthamstow might have been much smaller. The Domesday entry of 1086 shows that the northern parts formed a separate manor of Higham, (the High Home or enclosure – alternatively Higham Hill may have been Tunmanhille, or hill of the man of the settlement), but being more sparsely populated and not having their own church, the residents paid their tithes to Walthamstow church, and eventually these parochial ties anchored the northern manor to Walthamstow proper. The origin of the name Walthamstow is uncertain. It may be derived from Wilcume, an Anglo-Saxon woman's name or from *wicuma*, so that *Wicumastowe* would be 'the place where strangers were welcome', appropriate for the childhood home of William Morris, whose motto 'Fellowship is life' was adopted by the borough council, but just as likely wishful thinking by the etymologists of the mid twentieth century. Yet another possible origin for the name may come from the claim of Waltham Abbey to have founded the parish church. Take your pick.

There is archaeological evidence of human occupation dating back to the Stone Age, and in the Bronze and early Iron Age there were pile dwellings alongside the Lea on sites that are now under the reservoirs. Chingford takes its name from the Anglo Saxon 'Ford of the dwellers by the stumps', likely to be a reference to one of these pile dwelling sites. Remains from the Roman period have also been found, including a pot uncovered during the construction of Kingfisher Swimming Pool in 1933 alongside a small spring, but no substantial traces of buildings. The discovery of a log boat at Big Hill dating from about AD 950 confirms the antiquity of a ferry crossing of the Lea, but to date there has been no confirmation of the trackways that would have existed at the time of the Roman conquest and thereafter. The first documentary account of Walthamstow is from the Domesday survey of 1086, which forms our starting point to explore medieval farming and the manors.

Spade and Spur - the manors and their lands

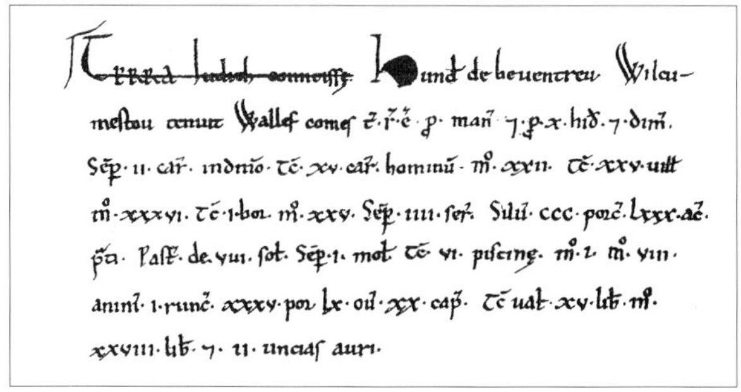

4. The Domesday entry for Walthamstow.

DOMESDAY, 1086

Domesday Walthamstow was divided into two manors. South of Chapel End was the manor of Wilcumstou and this later became Walthamstow Tony or High Hall. In 1066 it had formed part of the holdings of Waltheof, earl of Huntingdon, a Saxon who married Judith, the niece of William the Conqueror, in 1070. It consisted of the manor and ten and a half hides (later a hide in Essex came to approximate to 120 acres). After Waltheof's execution for plotting against the king in 1076, Judith succeeded to all her late husband's lands, but she was deprived of the honour of Huntingdon (which included the manor of Walthamstow) for refusing to marry Simon de Saint Liz, who acquired it instead through his marriage to Maud, Judith's daughter by Waltheof. Walthamstow passed to Maud's younger sister Alice when she married Ralph de Tony in 1106, and the de Tony family held it for the next two hundred years.

The de Tonys included an aspiring crusader, Ralph de Tony IV, who died on the way to the Holy Land in 1239. During the baronial struggles involving Simon de Montfort the manor was leased and by 1285 Adam de Bedyk held two carucates (depending on the quality of the soil, between 120 and 360 acres) in the south west. The lease persisted and the estate gained separate manorial status as the manor of Walthamstow Bedyk or Low Hall.

The northern manor of Higham and five hides of land were held by Haldan, a free man, in 1066 and by 1086 it was held in demesne – held directly by Peter de Valognes, the lord of the manor. One of the hides was added to the manor after the Conquest, and is probably the same land which Peter had taken from the chapter of St Paul's Cathedral, when it formed part of their manor of Chingford. Consisting of eight acres of meadow and some woodland, it later formed a detached part of Walthamstow parish inside Chingford, lying to the south of Chingford Hall. The de Valognes family held Higham manor until 1235, when it was divided between three sisters, Lora, the wife of Henry de Balliol, chamberlain of Scotland, Isabel, the wife of David Comyn and Christine, wife of Peter de Maul.

The two manors fared differently after the Conquest. Walthamstow (Tony) had two ploughs – and their oxen teams – in the demesne or lord's land and a further fifteen on the other lands, which had grown to 22 by 1086. The 25 villeins of 1066 had become 36 twenty years later, while the one bordar had been joined by a further twenty four. Villeins were of greater status than the bordars. They could hold as much as thirty acres of land, and would have had their own homestead – timber buildings surrounded by their own fence. Villeins owed services to the lord of the manor, but at other times would have farmed their own land. The Domesday villein could be a free man.

The bordar was the equivalent of the cottager, holding five acres of land at best and more often little more than a small plot of land around his house. He worked as a herdsman, labourer, or perhaps a craftsman, and would be bound to work on the demesne land at periods during the year. Serfs were unfree and Walthamstow has two for each of the lord's plough teams.

Walthamstow also had woods that supported 300 swine, 80 acres of meadow, pasture worth 8 shillings, one mill, which would have been water powered and on the Lea, and one fishery. There had been six in 1066. The livestock included a rouncey (horse), 35 swine, sixty sheep and twenty goats. The value of the manor had risen from £15 to £28 and two ounces of gold in 1086.

The smaller Higham manor had its own two ploughs for the demesne and four other teams in 1086. The eight villeins of 1066 had become ten, but two bordars had only risen to three. There was woodland for 300 swine, 18 acres of

5. The Ferry Boat Inn by the Lea river, where manor courts were held.

meadow, but the three and a half fisheries of 1066 had all gone. In 1066 Peter de Valognes had found just one ox and one acre of sown land. Twenty years on he had a manor that supported 15 beasts, one rouncey, 37 swine and two hives of bees. The value had risen from 60 shillings to four pounds and ten shillings, augmented by the additional land in Chingford parish, which had risen from 10s to 20s.

Some of these differences in the two manors can be explained by geography. The land that lay alongside the Lea in Higham's manor was high and unsuitable for pasture, and would normally have been marshland. Meadows were grassland, from which animals were excluded – usually from Candlemas, 2 February to Lammas on 1 August – so that the grass could be cut and dried for winter fodder. By the seventeenth century the equivalent Walthamstow dates were from Lady Day (25 March) to Midsummer Day (24 June). Walthamstow's meadow land may have corresponded to the later three commons – Church Common, and Markhouse Common and the southern part of Higham Hill common while the smaller Higham meadow lands may have been the northern part of Higham Hill common, which lay within that manor.

WOODLANDS

The forest area of Walthamstow and Higham manors may have been as much as 900 acres. On early nineteenth-century maps the old field boundaries showed a clear line that ran from Forest Road to the Leyton parish boundary, and this line may have marked the original limit of forest clearance from the Wood Street settlement, which may have existed at the time of Domesday. So by 1086 there had already been substantial land cleared of woodland. In the northern manor there were a number of fields with names derived from *braec*, the later 'brache', a clearance of woodland. Two were recorded in Higham Bensted in 1368, a 'Brache' of 62 acres and 'Shepecote Brache' of twelve acres. Later some of the original names became transformed by time – the most poetic of these being 'Cardmakers Braches'. Each of these represented the gradual erosion of the woodland as cultivated land was extended over the centuries. There are no firm dates for when these incursions took place, but at the Forest court of 1323-4 there were 17 presentments made for sowing corn in small enclosures and Walthamstow was one of the parishes that Charles I exacted payment in 1621 in return for a general grant of all land enclosed for cultivation in the past. So it is likely that the bulk of those enclo-

6. Gate to Markhouse Common, a view from the late 1860s.

sures in the southern manor had taken place by the end of the seventeenth century, after royal control had weakened, while to the north new enclosures were still being made in the eighteenth century, Woodland still survived between Hale End Road and Becontree Avenue in the eighteenth century and beyond Hale End over 190 acres were cut down between 1713 and 1748, leaving isolated forest groves among fields – such as Rowden, Salter's wood, and the larger areas of Great and Little Hale Brinks with a combined total of 44 acres. By 1843 outside the surviving forest and the estates of Highams, Belle Vue and the Hale Brinks woods, only thirteen acres of woodland remained.

MANORIAL CUSTOMS

The personal obligations of the manorial tenants to the lords of the manors were gradually commuted to monetary payments. By 1437 most of the labour services had their set charges – harrowing, weeding, hay making and work at the mill at a half penny each, harvesting tasks at 1d, reaping at 4d and ploughing at 8d. The values of these payments were then gradually eroded by inflation from the sixteenth century onwards. But the lords of the manor retained rights of control through the fines levied on land held of the manor (copyhold land), which descended by the custom of the Borough English, to the youngest son, or in default, by division amongst coheirs. These fines were not fixed by custom and kept pace with inflation.

The manors also exercised control over local farming practices. The three common arable fields remained divided into strips until 1850 and were rotated so that each in turn lay fallow for one year. In 1843 two thirds of these strips were less than an acre. In 1800 in the face of a shortage of corn, the parish passed a resolution allowing all three to be cropped.

Manorial common rights were also exercised over the marshes and the forest land. These could lead to disputes, as in the period 1587-91 when Thomas Rampston of Salisbury Hall tried to close the Broadmede gate against William Rowe of Higham Bensted and his tenants, to prevent them bringing hay from their holdings or driving cattle out. The marshes were also divided into strips and although rights of grazing from Lammas Day to Lady Day (September to March – Lammas rights), were extinguished on land needed for railway construction and for reservoirs, Lammas rights survived on over 100 acres until finally bought out by Walthamstow Council in 1938.

A ROYAL FOREST

Until 1878 Walthamstow was one of those Essex parishes that came within a royal forest – the forest of Waltham or Epping Forest. This had been created as a royal hunting reserve. Forest was a legal term – the landscape was a mixture of woodland and open space. But deer were to have free passage, and while enclosures could be made by royal licence, the hunt could cross such land with impunity, and the farmers and small holders could not prevent deer grazing on their land. Royal hunting was halted during the English Civil War and in 1653 parliament legislated to sell the entire Forest of Waltham, but the sale was held over pending an examination of how the land could best be used by the Commonwealth. Nothing had been decided at the Restoration of 1660, and Charles II resumed royal hunting rights, which finally lapsed with the accession of George I in 1714. However the Crown had also granted hunting rights to Londoners in the early medieval period, and this 'Epping Hunt' or ' Easter Chase' continued until 1882. In its later stages it was a great day out for Londoners.

To offset these losses, the inhabitants of parts of the forest parishes were granted rights over grazing and timber extraction. All manors except Salisbury Hall claimed selected common pasture rights on forest land for eleven months of the year. Sheep were excluded from these grazing rights, as they would have cropped the grass too closely to sustain deer. Cattle were also excluded from late June to late July, when fawns were born, and pigs could graze on the beech masts between 15 September and 8 November. The Domesday figures suggest that there may have been up to 600 pigs in the forest in these months. All cattle let loose were given special brands to identify them. In later years Walthamstow's mark was the letter 'O', topped by a crown. Marking was the responsibility of the parish reeve. Any unbranded cattle could be impounded and the owners of strays would be fined.

There were also claims made to rights of pollarding, gravel extraction and turf. Pollarding or lopping of trees started at midnight on 11 November and ended at midnight on 23 April each year. Oak, beech and fruit-bearing trees were excluded but others, including hornbeams could be cut above seven foot from the ground. But by 1865 people coming out from London were said to harass the cattle, while inclosures and gravel digging also affected grazing. The situation was stabilised by the Epping Forest Act of 1878, which preserved both forest and commoners' rights of pasturage, the subject of a later

7. Whipps Cross junction in 1861.

chapter. The Forest also provided wild animals and birds for the poor and the not so poor to poach, and a haven for outlaws and highwaymen.

DIVIDING THE MANORS

The two main manors were later subdivided. Adam de Bedyk, who died in 1302, tailor to the king, held an estate from the tenant of Walthamstow Tony in 1285, and this estate gradually separated from the main manor. It remained with the de Bedyk family until 1352 when it was sold to a London merchant, Simon Fraunceys. On Fraunceys' death six years later it was held jointly with his wife Maud from Thomas de Beauchamp, earl of Warwick, lord of Walthamstow Tony. By 1397 it had passed back into sole control of the earls of Warwick.

After the death of Henry de Beauchamp, earl of Warwick in 1446, both his Walthamstow manors passed first to his daughter, and then after her death three years later to her two aunts, Anne and Eleanor. Anne married Richard Neville, earl of Warwick who thus acquired Walthamstow Fraunceys, or Low Hall. Walthamstow Tony, passed to Eleanor and her husband Thomas de Ros. The de Ros succession was disrupted by the execution of Thomas de Ros, Lord Ros, for treason in 1464 and the manor was taken into royal hands until the accession of Henry VII in 1485. Edmund de Ros was abroad at the time and was later not judged to be trustworthy enough, so the family did not get it back. Instead the farm of his lands passed to his brother in law, Thomas Lovell, and after the death of de Ros without heirs in 1508, it was then leased. A succession of crown servants held it – firstly John Heron, master of the king's jewels, who also held land in Hackney, and who also leased Low Hall. Heron's son Giles inherited the lease, but was executed for treason in 1540, after which the Heron lands passed briefly to another trusted Crown servant, and one time Hackney resident, Ralph Sadleir, the builder of Sutton House. Sadleir exchanged it for other Crown lands in 1547.

The Ros family in the person of Henry Manners, earl of Rutland and Lord Ros, regained their former property in 1555. Through the marriage of his granddaughter descent passed to William Cecil, son of Lord Burleigh, who became the earl of Exeter. Their son, William Cecil, Lord Ros, came of age in 1611 and married Anne, daughter of Sir Thomas Lake, secretary of state, in 1616. In the following year scandal broke on the family, when Lady Ros accused the countess of Essex, the young wife of her husband's grandfather, of incest with her husband, and of attempting to poison her father and herself. To prove her case she forged letters and her brother, Arthur Lake, assaulted Ros, who fled abroad, and died there in 1618. The countess of Essex brought a defamation case against her accusers and both were found guilty. Much of Lady de Ros' property passed to the earl and countess, though she was able to recover the Walthamstow manor in 1623 when her new husband, George Rodney, paid the balance of her remaining debts.

Anne died in 1630 and George Rodney fought off claims of the Lake family to Walthamstow Tony, before selling it to Charles Maynard, an auditor of the exchequer. The Maynards, who owed their rise to the favour of the Burleigh family, were to retain the manor until the male line became extinct with the death of the last Viscount in 1865. His granddaughter Frances Maynard inherited and in 1881 married Francis Greville, Lord Brooke and later earl of Warwick.

Low Hall also passed to the Crown, seized by Edward IV after the death of the earl of Warwick at the battle of Barnet in 1471. It too was leased by the Heron family, and also passed to Ralph Sadleir, who retained it until 1560, when he sold it on to Thomas Argall. By descent it passed in the Argall family until Elizabeth Argall married Nathaniel Green, who were joint lords from 1701. Their heirs sold the manor to Samuel Bosanquet in 1741, whose descendants still owned it in 1926.

RECTORY MANOR

One other manor was taken from the Walthamstow Tony lands. This was the rectory manor, originating in a half virgate (about 15 acres) and an acre of meadow near the parish church, which was granted by Alice, daughter of Waltheof, to the priory of Holy Trinity, Aldgate, early in the twelfth century. It consisted of land lying between the present Church Hill and Forest Road and some other fields at Chapel End, on the marshes, and on Markhouse Common – by 1690 totalling some 72 acres. The title of the manor passed with the right to appoint to the rectory until 1638, when on the death of Lady Argall a sale of 1613 took effect and it passed to the Darell family. The last owner was Sir James Vallentin, who died in 1870. His trustees sold the estate for building in 1897, though the manorial rights were still vested in them in 1916.

8. *Henry Maynard.*

10. *Frances Evelyn Maynard, last of the Maynard family, and later Countess of Warwick.*

9. *Rectory Manor House.*

HIGHAM BENSTED

To the north the Higham manor had been divided between the three de Valognes sisters, Lora, Isabel and Christine, in 1235. One of the three shares, probably Lora's, came to make up land held by Alexander de Baliol, who sold it to John de Benstede, chancellor of the exchequer, in 1305, and the manor later became Higham Hill or Higham Bensted. The remaining two thirds, which lay principally between Billet Road and the Chingford boundary, were sold in 1323 to Adam of Salisbury, a London pepper merchant.

Helen de Benstede sold her manor to John Rysshe in 1493, though her title was disputed by Henry VII, whose servants ran the courts from 1494 to 1503, but in that year Rysshe's widow sold Higham Bensted to the Heron family, who lost it on the execution of Giles Heron in 1540. Again Ralph Sadleir appears in the story this time sub-letting some of the lands, and it is not surprising that the manorial tenants became confused as to just who their manorial lord was, so it is possible that in the 1550s some of the Higham Bensted holdings slipped away to the other Walthamstow manors.

Giles Heron's son Thomas got the manor back in 1554. The Herons sold it twelve years later to (Sir) Thomas Rowe, whose family held it for the next two hundred years until with a change in their fortunes, they sold it to Richard Newman in 1758. Later owners included William Hornby, a governor of Bombay (1785-90) and John Harman, a banker (1790-1817). Edward Warner bought it in 1849 and his heirs remain lords of the manor, playing a significant part in the development of the parish in the later nineteenth and early twentieth centuries.

SALISBURY HALL MANOR

The Salisbury family lost control of their manor in the early fifteenth century, and by 1450 it was held by Sir William Tyrwhitt, the builder of a chapel at Higham some six years earlier, from which the hamlet of Chapel End took its name. Sir Robert Tyrwhitt sold his manor to the Crown in 1541, who leased it out to various tenants until 1590. Among these was Roger Ascham, author of *The Scholemaster*, who was a Walthamstow resident from 1557 to his death in 1568. His widow Margaret married Thomas Rampston and the manor passed by inheritance and marriage to Robert Symonds in 1590. Symonds raised successive loans on the property in the 1590s, and may have rebuilt the manor house, but his son lost it through the foreclosure of a mortgage in 1649. Richard Edge bought it in 1657 and it passed by descent to the Rice Fellows family, who sold it to William Cooke in 1778. The Vale family owned it from 1817 to 1856, after which the Oliver family were lords until the last known member died in 1917.

THE MANOR OF MARK

There was a fifth manor in Walthamstow, the manor of Mark, which lay on the boundaries with Leyton, taking its name from the Anglo Saxon *mearc*, a boundary. Owned by St Helen's Priory in the late fifteenth century it passed to the Withypoll family after the dissolution of the monasteries. The estate was broken up in the late 1630s, and when the manorial rights were acquired by the Gansel family in the first half of the eighteenth century, they were united with the manor of Leyton.

MANORIAL LAW

The lord of the manor had a wide range of rights over his tenants, some of which later were taken over by the parish as it gradually assumed what we now think of as local government functions from the sixteenth century onwards. The manors

11. A modern map of Salisbury Hall and Higham Bensted manors, redrawn from the Coe map in 1920 by G.E. Roebuck. Salisbury Hall was the smaller manor, but its copyhold fields were scattered over the whole area of the map.

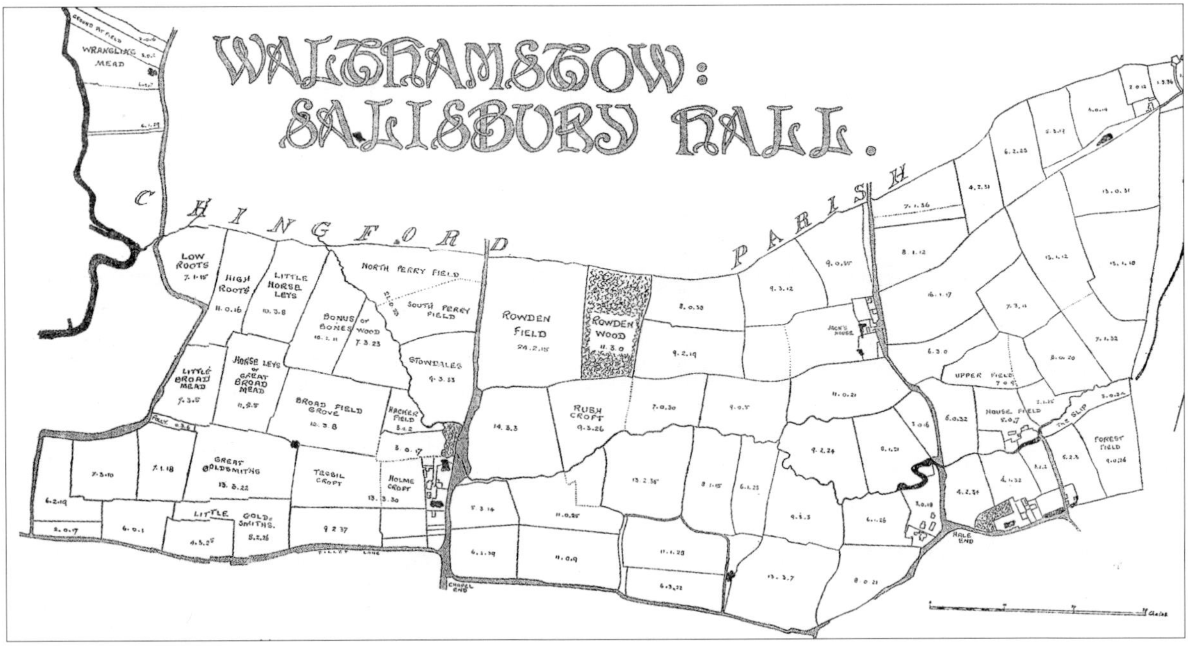

12. Roger Ascham, tutor to Queen Elizabeth.

had responsibility for law and order, and a gathering of tenants or 'view of frankpledge' in Walthamstow held by Ralph de Tony was recorded in 1278. In 1220 one Hugh Large of Walthamstow was accused of receiving two stolen horses from William Smallwood, the thief, who had murdered the chamberlain of Baldwin of Guines. Large was supposed to have kept them 'in his chamber' for eight days and received six shillings, while a woman at a nearby inn brought them water in secret, being paid 6d. Large was committed to the custody of the townsmen of Walthamstow until he and Smallwood were brought to a trial by combat, probably at Chelmsford, in which Large was the victor and Smallwood hanged. No exact locations are given for the 'chamber', but it is possible that Large's house was near the inn, that might have been a medieval precursor of the later Nag's Head, which stood opposite St Mary's Church.

In 1592 the quarter sessions presented the countess of Rutland for not maintaining a ducking stool and a pillory and in 1645 the constable was ordered to put up stocks and a whipping post, while the lord of the manor had to provide the pillory. On 29 April 1590 every householder in the manor of Higham Bensted was fined for not wearing caps on Sunday when going to the parish church – a breach of an Act of Parliament of 1571 which enjoined that everyone above the age of seven should wear 'a cap of wool knit thick and dressed in England made within this realm and only dressed and finished by some of the trade Cappers'. Maids, ladies, gentlemen, anyone holding land worth twenty marks and local office holders were all exempt. The fine was 3s, but on this occasion the lord of the manor seems to have waived it. A sterner position was taken with the constable for the northern manors in 1624. Constables were elected annually, and it was unfortunate that Robert White 'has kept in his house one Bridget Hide, an Harlot with whom the same Robert has committed fornication and of her begotten a male child and after its birth sent Bridget to places unknown'. That Robert had gone to some trouble to conceal his offence also rankled, and he was fined ten shillings.

Courts leet for the manor of Walthamstow Tony were held right up to 1895, and until 1881 elected constables and aleconners, although both posts were largely ceremonial by then. Manorial officials remained active in parish government up to the seventeenth century and retained control over Lammas lands and cattle pounds until the nineteenth century. But with one or two exceptions - such as in the 1740s when tenants were proceeded against for selling beer without a licence, the activities of the manor were mainly confined to rights of grazing and the transfer of copyhold land. By the mid nineteenth century this business was transacted at an annual court. Gilbert Houghton, born in 1853, attended as his father William's articled clerk and in his day the court was held at the Ferry Boat Inn, where after heirs had come forward, property sold and officials elected for the ensuing year, all sat down to a hearty dinner, with musical accompaniment. After all, the Ferry Boat was noted for its particularly fine wine cellar...

13. Belle Vue House, drawn by J. Hassell in 1817. The house was designed by Edward Gyfford for Charles Cooke and completed around 1803. Known as 'Cooke's Folly', it was set in landscaped grounds that included an irregular three-cornered lake. The estate, which lay to the west of Hale End Road, was sold for development in 1899, but Belle Vue survived on Hillcrest Road until 1937.

House and hamlet

So far we have taken something of a bird's eye view of the parish. This chapter takes us back to ground level and looks in turn at the hamlets, earlier dwellings and some of the people associated with them.

HALE END

As we have seen, Hale End was the most isolated part of the parish – the modern name of Highams Park comes from the Great Eastern Railway. The purchase of Highams lake and surrounding land by the Corporation of London from Sir Courtney Warner in 1891 prompted the railway company firstly to promote 'the most beautiful lake within a day's travel of London' and then change the station name from Hale End to Highams Park. In turn the station name was applied to the area, and although Hale End was tagged on to the station name after 1902, it was dropped again in 1969.

The smaller of the two villages in the northern manor of Higham Bensted, the core of Hale End was round the Royal Oak, where three roads met. But when the northern manor was divided into two, the manor house for the eastern manor was built at Chapel End, attracting its own small settlement, and ensuring that there was little expansion of Hale End to the west. Round it were additional areas of cleared land, and their associated farm buildings – Nightingale Hall close to Chingford Hatch, Stretmans, near the present Vincent Road and Hungry Hall or Jack's House, later the site of the British Xylonite works on Larkshall Road. Hungry Hall takes its name from the Anglo-Saxon *hangra,* a wood growing on a slope, and the alias is from John Jack, a tenant of the farm in 1505. Between Jack's Farm and the village of Hale End was Wadham Farm, bequeathed by John Goodridge to his own college, Wadham College, Oxford, in 1652, and which the college held until 1894, after which it was sold to dairyman John Hitchman, whom we shall encounter again.

There was a 'Benstedes' manor house which probably stood near the present Higham Park station from the thirteenth century, and it is mentioned in 1306 and again in 1368. The site is now lost, though Coe's map has a Benstedes field

14. Jack's House at Hale End.

near Jack's Farm, which may commemorate the building.

Although there was no later manor house at Hale End, Stretman's was sometimes given that title. By 1433 it was home to the de Hale family (later simply the Hales), who were once the wealthiest of the local inhabitants. By the early sixteenth century they also owned Scotts, which John Hale left to his son John in his will of 1521. Named after an early sixteenth-century tenant John Scott, this lay on the south side of Hale End Road, near the village centre. However the fortunes of the Hale family suffered a reversal, for they held to the Catholic faith in the face of the Tudor reformation, and Thomas Hale and Ann his wife had the misfortune to be the first recusants to be presented at the Essex quarter sessions in 1583. On his death in 1591 Thomas still owed £100 in unpaid fines and had written to the Privy Council six years previously explaining that he had less than 5s in money and his plate was worth less than four marks. All these farms were rebuilt in the eighteenth century. There is no record of their earlier appearance, but they would have been timber frame buildings, covered with wattle and daub, with brick chimneys added from the sixteenth century onwards.

A little to the south of Hale End was Thorpe Hall, on the west side of Hale End Road, roughly on the line of the junction with the modern Thorpe Hall Road. Thorpe Hall may have been the home of George Gascoigne, (*c.*1539-1577), MP, poet and soldier, who is recorded as living in Walthamstow in 1564. Gascoigne married well, but his wife had already been promised to someone else and it took a lengthy court case before Gascoigne could enjoy his wife and her property. But a period as a farmer was not a success, and in 1570 he spent time in Bedford Gaol for debt. After three years in Holland, the poet returned to England in 1574 and wrote pieces for a royal progress through Warwickshire, but just when his life seemed to

15. George Gascoigne.

16. Beech Hall at Hale End. Watercolour by Annie R. Hatley, 1930. Standing on the west side of the Hale End junction. Beech Hall, originally a farmhouse, was dated before 1782. Home of Edward Forster the younger, noted botanist, from 1816-26, it was demolished in 1930.

be on the mend he was struck down by disease and died in Lincolnshire in 1577. Gascoigne's stepson was Nicholas Breton, another Elizabethan poet, part of whose childhood would have been spent at the Walthamstow house.

CHAPEL END

West of Hale End lay Chapel End, around the cross roads now under the Crooked Billet roundabout. The earliest house in this area was Water Hall, first mentioned in 1286, when it was held by William de Betoyne, later a Sheriff of London and a City MP. This has been identified with the property later known as Moons Farm, once a large moated building, originally E- shaped, but reduced in size in the seventeenth century. The later name is from George Monoux, the Walthamstow benefactor who bought it in 1513 along with Chapel Longlands, later four fields which formed the area lying between Brookscroft Road, Chingford Road and Wadham Road. The farm buildings stood on the site of Monoux Grove and lasted until 1927.

Salisbury Hall manor house was almost certainly built shortly after the de Salisbury family acquired the manor in 1322. The site lay just south of the Ching river, with outbuildings to the west, and looked south towards the crossroads. It was timber framed built on chalk block and Kentish ragstone foundations and measured about fifty feet long by thirty feet wide. There were three rooms on the front, measuring roughly 14ft by 18ft. A narrow strip of gravel across the front suggested that the original building was moated.

This house formed the nucleus for the new settlement. The original name may have been Rodon End – in 1501 the gallows and pillory there were ordered to be repaired – and this name may have derived from *ruh dun*, a rough hill or valley. Rowden Field and Rowden Wood lay on the east side of Chingford Road, and the name survives in the present Rowden Road. The change of name arose from the activities of Sir William Tyrwhit, lord of the manor, who in 1422 built a chantry chapel of St Edward 'for the souls of King Henry V and VI and for his own soul and the souls of his deceased parents Robert Tyrwhit and Alice his wife and of John Portyngton and Helen his wife and of Thomas Portyngton and Alice his wife, parents of the said John Portyngton'. This chapel was built on a site about 350 yards east of Chingford Road and 70 yards north of Wadham Road. A driftway passed it to the east, and the

17. Salisbury Hall. Pen and ink drawing by Dennis Flanders, 1937.

field to the south became Higham Chapel Broadfield. All chantries were suppressed in 1547 and Sir William's foundation was left to fall down.

The original Salisbury Hall was destroyed by a fire in the early sixteenth century – small drops of lead found in the gravel at the front of the house would have been molten when they dropped into the moat round the house. There may have been a period when the site was uninhabited, for the brickwork used in the second house dates from the mid sixteenth century, and it was built a little to the south on the site of the former moat. The core of the house measured fifty foot by twenty foot and was divided into three rooms. There were two main stories and additional rooms in the attic. A small extension was added to the west, and another to the north end, built between 1680 and 1730. The timber frame and wattle and daub structure rested on a foundation of dwarf bricks, and the older part had a central brick chimney stack, while there were brick ovens at the west end. At the rear was an enclosed well, which dated back to the original medieval house.

The likely first occupant of the new house, as a tenant of the Crown, was Robert Ascham (*see p. 16*), who leased the manor in 1557. Ascham (b1515) became a Professor of Greek at Cambridge, wrote a treaty on archery, and in 1548 became tutor to the young Princess Elizabeth. He prospered under Queen Mary and became her Latin Secretary by 1555. In 1563-8 he wrote his best known work, *The Scholemaster,* some of which would have been written at Salisbury Hall. After his death in 1568 his widow Margaret married Thomas Rampston, who in the course of asserting his rights involved himself in a number of disputes with his tenants. When a manorial jury refused to give him the decision he wanted over a new gateway, he and his steward Francis Grenham 'locked them up in a verye narrowe roome and threatened to keepe them fasting untill they gave direct verdict as they commanded'.

The jury proved obdurate and were twice confined and threatened with proceedings at the Star Chamber, prison and a fine of £10 per person and of the loss of their copyhold. Rampston also disputed the rights over two fields with the neighbouring manor of Higham Bensted and in 1587 also became embroiled in a dispute over a field gateway.

The site of Great Broadmead field is now under

18. *Moons Farm c.1920.*

19. *Higham Hill house, seen in its reduced state in an engraving dated 1756.*

the Banbury reservoir, but in the 1580s local people had rights of access to cut hay and afterwards pasture cattle. There was an existing field gateway near the point where Folly Lane bends north again (near the junction with the modern Durban Road) but in 1586 Thomas Rampston closed this gate up and set up another. He was opposed by the tenants of Higham Bensted manor and their lord William Rowe, and when the tenants tried to bring out their hay a fight ensued in which one of Rowe's men broke Rampston's head. A Star Chamber case followed, but whatever the verdict it would seem that the gateway stayed in its old position

Margaret Rampston died around 1590 and the manor then passed to her daughter Anne, who married Robert Symonds. Symonds mortgaged the property and may have been responsible for further building work. The house was described as 'mean' in 1768, but survived until 1952, when its status as an ancient monument was not enough to protect it from demolition. An extensive excavation undertaken during 1953-55 provided considerable archaeological evidence about the house and its predecessor. The site later became part of the car park of the Walthamstow dog stadium.

HIGHAM HILL

The original settlement at Higham Hill would have been near the junction of Billet Road and Blackhorse Road. The original manor house, called Waterhall by 1368 may have been Moons Farm. However there was also a house at the core of the settlement, known later as Higham Hill. By the sixteenth century this was used as the manor house and was extensively rebuilt by William Rowe between 1570 and 1596. The resulting property was around 100 foot long and 76 foot deep. Three stories high, the house also had its own chapel with the arms of William Rowe and his wife inlaid into the wainscoting. After Rowe's death his widow married Sir Reginald Argall, already lord of the Rectory Manor. His brother John Argall inherited, and his wife and later widow, Dame Anne lived there until her death in 1638. Thereafter the house passed back to the Rowe family, but their fortunes gradually declined. Around 1683 one storey of the house was taken down and by 1756 the antiquarian and family member Edward Rowe Mores commented 'since that time it has been much reduced: the magnificent hall and other spacious apartments on the east have in late years been entirely demolished, [about 1730] so that at present the west

20. Essex Hall in the 1920s. The stable block alongside was used by the Misses Cooper as their schoolroom.

end only of the fabric is remaining and that so strangely deformed by an artless contriver as to retain little or no resemblance of what it formerly was'. Some of the building materials were recycled for other use – woodwork from the chapel went to repair some small houses on Marsh Street. In 1762 the manor was sold separately.

No longer the manor house, Higham Hills was divided into two. By the early nineteenth century it became Essex Hall and was used by the Rev Eliezar Cogan as a school. In 1861 it was leased to the Cooper family, who later bought it from the Rowes. The Misses Cooper used the Cogan's schoolrooms as a Sunday school. The house and its ground were acquired by Walthamstow Council to build council housing after the First World War, and Essex Hall was finally demolished in about 1934. In 1970 the Essex Hall old people's home stood on the site.

The medieval court records give seven houses in the Higham Hill area in the fifteenth century. Mundaynes tenement stood at the junction of the modern Lawrence Avenue and Billet Road until around 1642. Byrdes was on the site of Romany Gardens and another, unnamed, house on the site of Garnett Way. Both were acquired by the parish in 1691 with money arising from the will of Sir Henry Maynard. Byrdes was demolished, and the combined property and land formed Bulls Farm. South of Billett Road was Acremans (in the angle between Higham Hill and Billett roads), demolished in 1559, after which a barn was built on the site. Also on the south side of Billet Road were Admunds between nos. 275 and 291 (demolished after 1666), another unnamed house on the sites of nos 38-60 Billet Road until the late seventeenth century, a house called the Mile End and a last unnamed property on the land between Sinnot, Sutton and Billet roads, which lasted until 1781.

George Monoux also piped his drinking water from a spring at Higham Hill, probably from a source just north of Gloucester Road. In 1528 John Webb, a tenant of Low Hall manor, granted Monoux a licence to take water from Caryswell, and 'Edify and build a conduit house with stone and timber' near the well. A course of hollowed-out tree trunks then carried the water to Moons Farm, some of which were still intact four hundred years later when Moons was demolished.

South of Higham Hill on the site of the present junction of Tavistock and Pembar avenues was High Hall. This may have served as the Walthamstow Tony manor house and is mentioned in 1483. George Rodney, then lord of the manor, probably sold it separately from the manor between 1612 and 1629. It is shown on the Forbes map of the manor of 1699. By 1768 it was a handsome brick farmhouse and six years later was bought by the Quaker Lewis Weston, who considerably enlarged it. To the south on Blackhorse Road was Higham Lodge, probably built in the late seventeenth century but also enlarged by Weston's friend and fellow Quaker William Dilwyn, whose grandfather had accompanied William Penn to America in 1699. Dilwyn married Weston's daughter in 1777 and the combination of the two estates led eventually to the demolition of High Hall in 1834. Higham Lodge survived to become part of Baird and Tatlock's scientific instrument making works (from 1902). Despite becoming a listed building the house was demolished in the 1980s.

There were also a number of cottages on Blackhorse Road. The Blue Cottages stood near the site of the Blenheim Road junction from before 1781 until they were demolished in 1898/9. On the site of Blackhorse Road station were cottages known as Dutch Place. And along Forest Road west of the Higham Hill Road junction were a group of wooden cottages known as Little Dublin, one of which served as an unlicensed

21. William Dilwyn in 1833. From a drawing by E.U. Eddis, engraved by Gauchi.

22. The Blue Cottages near the site of Blenheim Road, in 1897.

beerhouse run by Joseph Dell in 1750, and known as the Leather Bottle until it came to the attention of the manorial court. Built in the seventeenth century the last of these buildings survived into the early twentieth century.

FOREST ROAD

Further along the Clay Street part of the present Forest Road a house called the Priory stood on the site of nos. 361-379 . It was probably an eighteenth-century house, enlarged in 1809-11, given a fashionable sounding name, perhaps drawing an association with Prior's Street, the sixteenth-century name for part of Forest Road. Further west lies the present William Morris Gallery, also known as Water House. This was an ancient moated site known variously as Winns, Cricklewood, Hawks Capp or Winns Cap. There was a house there in the 1630s, when it was home to Sir Thomas Merry, a supporter of the Royalist cause in the Civil War. When his wife died in 1632, Sir Thomas commissioned a family memorial from Nicholas Stone, master mason to Charles I. It shows Dame Mary, Sir Thomas and their four children, and the verses on the memorial have been attributed to Sir William Davenant. Sir Thomas lived on until 1654, so he had over twenty years of attending church and gazing on his own marble effigy.

After Merry's death the house was the residence of William Pierse, Bishop of Bath and Wells, who on his death in Walthamstow in 1670 aged 94 was said to be the oldest bishop in Christendom. Winns was the home of Ralph Hawkins, a London brewer in 1684, later passing to William Woolball, who had lived at Grosvenor House in Hoe Street, and then to his daughter Catherine, who married Sir Hanson Berney. The house was let to Peter Lefevre, a West Ham distiller, who died in 1751. In the marriage settlement for Catherine Woolball the house, supposedly still in the occupation of Lefevre, was described as newly built, so it is likely that Sir Thomas Merry's house had been extensively altered in the 1740s. The cellar of the present house does not wholly correspond with the room layout above and may have been retained from the older property.

To the east of the Forest Road junction with Hoe Street is Brookscroft, on the south side of Forest Road. The present house dates from 1762-3, and its first owner was George Hayley, but Brokkys Croft, a twelve-acre field was so named in 1475 when John Badley occupied it. A house stood there in 1568, lived in by the Sawier family which had held the field since 1531. Described as tiled in 1578 it was demolished in 1759.

23. The Water House in Forest Road, at one time the home of the family of William Morris. At the time of this picture it was called Winns.

24. Wood End House in Wood Street. A watercolour c.1850.

In the land bounded by Forest Road, Shernhall Street, Wyatt's Lane and the northern end of Wood Street there were once three eighteenth-century houses, two of which survive. Thorpe Combe was built on Catchers Field, probably for Richard Manby a City of London bookseller in 1762. Walthamstow House on Shernhall Street, dates from between 1750 and 1760, and sited so that in 1804 it was said to command views north almost to Hatfield. This house had a long association with the Wigram family, of whom more later. The third house, Wood End House, was on the west side of Wood Street, just north of the Wyatt's Lane junction. An older house that existed in 1676, then owned by Thomas Fleming, passed eventually to Sarah Littlepage and her cousin John Perry, who obtained manorial consent to knock it down in 1771. A new house was completed by 1773, and became the home of Captain William Money after 1780, who will also be encountered later, in company with the Wigrams.

WOOD STREET

Wood Street itself lay in a valley, roughly three quarters of a mile long. There were twenty names in the rate roll of 1676, most towards the northern end, but a smaller group down by Whipps Cross. By 1822 Wood Street down to the junction with Church Lane was lined with timber-framed cottages and shops, and eighteen years later was home to some of the poorest in Walthamstow. Among the alleys and courts was the now vanished Jeffreys Square, to the south of the Duke's Head, demolished in 1931-4. This may have been named from a prosperous retired London butcher, Joseph Jeffries, who was murdered by his niece

25. Wood Street with the Plough public house on the left. A woodcut of c.1785.

26. The rear of the houses in Jeffreys Square, looking north. Watercolour by T. Stuart Milner, 1933. The modern Marlowe Road is on the other side of the houses on the left of the picture.

and her accomplice in 1751, and who lived in a house further north. Just east of the site of Jeffreys Square, no. 114 Wood Street is the last surviving timber framed house in the road. Inside a central chimney stack is surrounded by two rooms upstairs and two on the ground floor, plus what was once a lean-to scullery.

Wood Street also has a long history of taverns. Six cottages south of Wyatts Lane included one that became the Duke's Head (first mentioned as such in 1742), while an L-shaped house on the site of Woodlands Road was the Thatched House, a seventeenth-century tavern, later the Hornes, then after 1710 a private house whose name transmuted to Homes, before being renamed the Woodlands. After the passing of drinking at the Hornes, trade shifted to a cottage on the site of Wood Street station, which became the Plough and Harrow, later simply the Plough. From the early eighteenth century drinkers could also retire to the Old Buck, a small beerhouse near the site of Buck Walk, whose sign showed a buck jumping over a house – perhaps it was something to do with the beer.

There were four houses at Whipps Cross in 1676. The survivor is Clock House, which stands on the site of an older house called Wat Webbes, which was demolished by the occupier, Arthur Bayley, between 1683 and 1706. This house or cottage, occupied by Richard Webbe in 1478, may have dated back to the early fourteenth century, as members of the Webbe family appear on taxation rolls for this part of Walthamstow in 1327 and 1332. Bayley's new house, which took it name from the clock on the stable block, passed to Jacob Jacobson in 1713. Jacobson, a London merchant, planted an avenue of trees along a drive opposite the house – once the line of the present Woodside Park Avenue – and had a series of fishponds dug to the south, stretching down to Whipps Cross, known later as 'Sir Jacob's Water' or 'Sir Jacob's fishponds'. The one dug at the east end of the drive still survives in the garden of a private house.

Jacobson was also a director of the South Sea Company and when the frenzied financial speculation in the company's shares ended in the crash of 1720, his was one of the estates confiscated by the government to provide partial relief to ruined investors. Jacobson was able to buy back the bulk of it in 1724, though two acres of land he held on Church Common were sold on. One of these was bought by Walthamstow parish in 1729 and became the site of the parish workhouse. After the death of Jacobson in 1736 and his wife, Dame Anne two years later, the property was bought

27. Rear view of Clock House, 1862. This and the other three watercolours of Clock House which follow were drawn when the house was lived in by the Morgan family, who had moved in shortly before 1861 and are probably by a family member. David Thomas Morgan was a member of the Walthamstow local board, and his son David John Morgan (1844-1918) was MP for the Walthamstow division of Essex from 1900-06. The house was bought by Walthamstow Borough Council in 1938 and converted into flats.

28. The drawing room of Clock House in 1862.

29 & 30. Watercolours of Clock House in 1862. Above the cedar room, below the dining room.

by her nephew, Alderman George Heathcote, who served as Lord Mayor of London in 1742 and lived there until 1744. The Heathcotes had been a Wood Street family from the early eighteenth century – Anne Jacobson's brother, Sir Gilbert Heathcote, one of the founders of the Bank of England and Lord Mayor of London in 1710, had been resident there. Reputed to be the richest commoner in England – and the meanest – Heathcote had bought the nearby Forest House estate in Leyton in 1703.

Clock House was rebuilt in its present form early in the nineteenth century by Jesse Russell. To the east of Wood Street Buck Lane ran north of Buck House to Sir John Salter's houses, which faced east on to the forest and consisted originally of a single five-bay house called Forest Hall and a semi-detached pair. By the early nineteenth century these had become a row. All were demolished in the 1930s. Eastwards again is a row of Georgian houses, the earliest of which dates from about 1760, which now comprise Forest School.

SHERNHALL STREET

In contrast to Wood Street, Shernhall Street had few houses in the early nineteenth century south of the junction with Church Lane. Winchester House, on the west side of the road by Church Lane was built in 1768 (demolished 1960) and Shern Hall Lodge opposite just south of the Vallentin Road junction, was built in 1760 and demolished in 1966. The oldest house in the road was Shern Hall, which stood on the east side to the south of the present Barrett Road junction. The great eastern bend Shernhall Street takes went round the original estate, which included a large T-shaped lake, with the top and longest part of the T on the alignment on the present

31. Winchester House in Shernhall Street about 1870, when the house was occupied by the Livingstone family. Jaspar Livingstone was aged 53 and a ship and engine broker. He had been born in Jamaica. The group included his wife Mary, also 53 in 1871, and possibly his sister-in-law Georgina Shuttleworth. There were three servants. A view from the Houghton family album.

32. Pen and ink drawing of Shernhall Street. The sign of the Lord Brooke public house is on the right.

Greville Road. There had been a 'chief mansion house' here in 1636, when Charles Maynard bought the manor from George Rodney, and this may be the two-storey ten-bay house, with attic dormers which is shown on the 1699 Walthamstow Tony manor map. Shern Hall probably dated from no earlier than the beginning of the seventeenth century and was gradually altered by successive occupiers so that by the mid nineteenth century it had been reduced in size, and the brick covered by stucco. One famous nineteenth-century tenant was Dr (later Cardinal) Wiseman. Shern Hall was damaged in a fire of 1879, but the house was demolished in 1896 and its surviving grounds were built over shortly afterwards.

CHURCH HILL

West from Shernhall Street Church Lane led to the church and Church Hill – now at the heart of the modern 'Walthamstow Village'. Facing St Mary's Church is the Ancient House, which may be on the site of Walthamstow's first manor house. The second, recent, restoration of the Ancient House has shown that the original timber work

33. South view of Shern Hall.

34. The Ancient House with full timber cladding. A watercolour of about 1870 by J.T. Wilson

35. After many transformations, the Ancient House is undergoing another, intended to restore an appearance deemed to be more authentic. Drawing by Butler and Hegarty, architects, 2001.

36. Beams and uprights exposed during the restoration of the Ancient House in 2000. Photograph, Gary Heales.

dates from between 1430 and 1440. It may be the property mentioned in the will of William Hyll, vicar of Walthamstow from 1470-87 as 'a tenement of myne called John Kykylwoldys'. Originally it consisted of a single central hall and just the east wing, whose framing would have been designed for display from Church Lane. The west wing dates from around 1580, and is likely to have been added as a service wing. There are likely to have been more alterations in the early 1720s, when the house was owned by John Ash of Hackney and by 1757 when it passed to Theophilus Green it was divided into two houses. Green sold off 14.5 acres of land behind the house and, without its associated estate, the Ancient House was bought by Richard Cooke, who may have been the landlord of the Nag's Head. The heir of the last surviving Cooke sold it to Elizabeth Lucking in 1811, and the house was then further sub-divided into four tenements, later becoming shops. An extensive restoration of 1934 included pitch and tar additions to the original oak, which raised moisture content, and led to wet rot decay. The major work undertaken in 2000-2001 revealed more about the history of the house and will lead to a different kind of reconstruction, based more on what the house might have looked like, but retaining the weatherboarding on the east end. The 1930s tan and black look will be replaced by wattle and daub, covered with a lime render, bringing back to Walthamstow the 'White House', as the Ancient House was known in the eighteenth century.

The vacant space on the other side of Orford Road was the site of the original Nag's Head, demolished in 1859, when the licence was transferred to the present building on Orford Road, as 'The house having become by unforseen and unavoidable calamity unfit for the reception of travellers'. A grocer's shop which replaced the inn lasted for exactly a hundred years before it was demolished in 1959. On the other side of Church Lane the path to the church was once flanked by two sets of three cottages, known as the Parish House, and held by the churchwardens for the use of the parish poor. One site dated from before 1565 and the other from around 1670. In 1708 Walthamstow acquired a new and very active vicar, Edmund Chishull, who regarded the cottages as encroachments on the churchyard. He had the back doors stopped up in 1713, probably under the pretext of preventing the occupants dumping their rubbish in the churchyard and then insured that the inhabitants should have first call on a place in a parish almshouse. The eastern range was in poor repair and as soon as the last inhabitant had moved out the remains of all three cottages were cleared in June 1721. Two of the three tenants of the western range were found to have no rights to be there, the third was moved to an almshouse and the second set of cottages went in November 1721. Technically the parish should have sought manorial permission to knock the cottages down, but perhaps no-one wanted to take on a very determined vicar.

The parish church, almshouse and schools will be covered in later chapters. No. 10 Church Lane was built on the Ancient House's former garden in 1830. The Chestnuts, which now fronts on to the modern Bishop's Close, may date back to the early nineteenth century – the grounds were south and east of the house. On the other side of the road, the Walnuts stood immediately east of the churchyard. This house was used by J.F.Roberts, headmaster of Monoux School, as a residence and for boarding pupils from 1820-1835, after which he moved to the Chestnuts. The house, which had been latterly the residence of the Bishop of Barking, was demolished in 1937.

Rectory manor house was on the north side of Church Hill on land known as Parsonage Hill. There was a house there in 1530, which had been demolished by 1690. A new house was built in 1762 by John Watson and was enlarged for a later tenant by Sir John Soane in 1783, with later works in 1791. It was to Rectory manor house that Sir James Vallentin moved after Shern Lodge's grounds were bisected by the railway in the late 1860s and eventually it was his trustees who sold the house and the estate for building development in 1897, after which the house was rapidly demolished. Opposite Church Hill House, on the eastern corner of the later junction with Folkestone Road and built in 1784, lasted until 1934. The door case was saved and added to the former armoury part of Vestry House Museum. To the south of the village and originally separated from it by Church Common is Orford House, which was built between 1800 and 1822 and is now a social club.

37. The Walnuts, Church Lane. Watercolour by Bernard Bowerman, 1937.

38. Church Hill House. From the Houghton album, c.1870.

HOE STREET

The land around Hoe Street south of the junction with High Street mostly belonged to the Conyers family in 1699. Tristram Conyers built a house on the east side around 1600, later named Grosvenor House. It had its own avenue lined by elms leading to Church Common; this later became the present Grosvenor Park Road. After the mid eighteenth-century occupation of William Woolball, the Grosvenor family owned it and had it rebuilt in white Suffolk brick about 1789. It was refronted sometime before 1796 and lasted until 1945 when it was gutted in a fire, and the shell demolished eleven years afterwards.

To the south there were two other large houses. The Chestnuts, opposite Grove Road, stands on the site of an earlier house, owned by Lancelot Staveley in 1660. Staveley's widow married John Claypoole, whose late wife had been Elizabeth Cromwell one of Oliver Cromwell's daughters. The Chestnuts was extensively rebuilt by Thomas Allen in 1747. Allen lived in the old and new house from 1743 to 1763. It is now a large two storey seven-bay house and has a three-bay central pediment. The porch was added in the nineteenth century. The house still has a paved hall, an open well staircase with turned balusters and decorated plasterwork. Among the later occupants were the Bosanquets, lords of the manor of Low Hall and the Berthon family.

Peter Berthon had been making a good living in the Napoleonic Wars as an army supplier. In 1816 a convoy carrying Berthon's goods was wrecked at just the moment when the effects of the peace treaty signed at the Congress of Vienna took effect. Berthon lost his contracts, and the

39. Grosvenor House in Hoe Street, 1792.

40. Court House in Hoe Street.

41. The Red House, from the Houghton album, probably about 1875.

drop in income led to an abrupt change of house – a move to the smaller Court House, which stood near the junction with Grove Road. Peter Berthon's son Edward, then aged three, remembered the move some eighty years later in which he had dragged his toy cart across the road, 'and how we wondered to see mamma and our elder sisters all crying.' The Chestnuts continued to be home to bankers and merchants until 1891. In the early twentieth century it served as a branch lunatic asylum for Essex, before seeing successive use for a variety of educational uses. Court House itself, a five bay house dating back to about 1700 was bomb damaged in World War II and demolished in 1952. The Red House projected out into Hoe Street just north of Grove Street and was a casualty of post-war road widening. Built in 1785, and home to a number of prosperous families, including the Houghtons, local solicitors and estate agents, it was demolished in 1963.

Clevelands House, to the south of the Orford Road junction is another survivor. In its present form it is a tall and narrow early eighteenth-century building, rebuilt in 1760, which has been refronted and had wings added, which were raised in 1871. The name comes from an unproven association with Barbara Villiers, mistress of Charles II and Duchess of Cleveland, though the most notable known residents were the Forster family, with scientific and horticultural interests.

43. Edward Forster the younger (1765-1849), botanist and philanthropist. Lithograph from a drawing by T.H. Maguire, 1849.

MARSH STREET

The earliest houses on Marsh Street – the name did not change to High Street until December 1882 – were in the section between the modern Palmerston and Blackhorse roads. Besides a number of small cottages there was a larger house here – the Black House from which Blackhorse Lane took its name. The site was taken for Clock House, built for Thomas Courtney Warner (*see p. 40*). At the east end on the north side was a group of four large houses in the 1660s, with gardens running back parallel with Hoe Street. The corner house was owned by Admiral William Batten, and the adjoining one by his fellow

42. Houses in Marsh Street, 1860.

Admiral, William Penn. The diarist Samuel Pepys visited both men and in 1661 was present when Batten 'did give the company that were there a bottle or two of his own last year's wine, growing at Walthamstow, than which the whole company said they never drank better foreign wine in their lives'. A choice Walthamstow vintage then. Batten died in 1667, but his widow remarried and lived on at the house.

Batten's neighbour, William Penn's son was the founder of Pennsylvania, but he also had a daughter Margaret, who married Antony Lowther, who owned land in the vicinity of the present Town Hall on Forest Road. The newly married couple attracted local gossip which Pepys picked up on ' ... how the parish talks of Sir W.Pen's family, how poorly they cloathe their daughter so soon after the marriage, and do say that Mr Lowther was married once before .... But to think of the clatter they make with his coach and his own fine clothes and yet how meanly they live within doors, and nastily and borrowing everything of neighbours.' Penn died in 1670

In the most westerly of these four houses the occupant was Dr Daniel Whistler, who in 1665 had married Lowther's widowed mother. He was the first man to identify rickets as a disease. Penn and Batten's houses were demolished at the end of the seventeenth century and replaced by a row of four smaller ones. The third of these newer houses was owned by a wealthy London merchant, William Coward. The E- shaped house was on the site of the present Westbury Road, with its lower side parallel with Marsh Street. Coward was to become a prominent patron of the local nonconformist community and the first Walthamstow meeting house was built at the bottom of his garden in 1695. After his death in 1738 his house was demolished and two new houses were built on the part of the garden fronting the road, known later as the Ivy House and Chestnuts or Gillards. A short distance to the west of the site of Coward house a new house, yard and stables appeared around 1740, and this was to be the site of Joseph Schooling's coaching business.

On the opposite side of the road and taking up the eastern part of the site of the present shopping centre was a large house called Butlers Place (also Lambes or Cups), which was built prior to 1605, which also passed into the ownership of William Coward around 1712. Other substantial houses included Norcotts, on a site later occupied by Woolworths, which was built before 1744, rebuilt in 1761 and demolished in 1965. Clevelands, later no. 263 High Street, may have been altered and enlarged by John Soane for James Neave in 1781-3, though it retained a panelled interiors and staircase dating back to around 1700. It served as the local education offices before being demolished in August 1959 prior to the construction of the shopping arcade and the post office on Hoe Street. On the corner of Erskine Road was a house built a little after 1717, and owned in 1737 by William Snell, an attorney and another mainstay of the local nonconformist community.

44. The Chestnuts in Marsh Street.

45. The Chequers, c.1968, once the venue for vestry gatherings.

46. Clock House in Pretoria Avenue, 2001.

Standing back from the High Street, and now on the corner of Pretoria Avenue and Mission Grove is the Clock House. Built shortly after 1813 for Thomas Courteney Warner. As mentioned earlier, it is on the site of the Black House, which had its own substantial grounds, totalling six acres, and an entrance lodge on Marsh Street. Warner had the lot demolished and his new house built in Suffolk White bricks. It also had a lodge on the Marsh Street side and fine entrance gates. As built the house had a bay window on the east side and a fine columned portico entrance. The Warners moved out in 1847, when they acquired the Highams estate and manor, and after the construction of shops in that area of the High Street the entrance gates were moved to Highams. The grounds were later sold off, and by 1913 the house was wholly boxed in by terraced houses. Today Mission Grove cuts across the frontage, but the house survives and in June 2001 was in the course of restoration work.

At the corner of St James Street was a large house, whose ground ran back westwards down the south side of Coppermill Lane. In 1809 this was owned by Richard Abbey, a wholesale tea merchant, whose business was near Cheapside. In 1814 Abbey became one of the guardians of John Keats the poet, and his sister Fanny, then aged 11. Fanny went to live with the Abbeys in Walthamstow and the City, but she was kept isolated and was very lonely. On her 21st birthday in 1824, after the early death of her brother, Fanny was at last able to escape, and never returned. On the opposite side of the road, the last of the larger houses was the Elms, a seventeenth-century house, demolished in 1968, whose site now forms part of the ground of the Douglas Eyre Centre. Eighteenth-century occupiers included Antony Todd, Secretary of the Post Office 1762-98 and after Todd's death William Matthew Raikes, nephew of Robert Raikes, founder of the Sunday school movement. Both Todd and W.M. Raikes were trustees of the Lea Bridge and Road Trust.

There were also cottage properties along Marsh Street. One group in the vicinity of the present Erskine and Palmerston roads in the late seventeenth century included a house which was to become the Chequers public house. This became one of the places of business favoured by those

47. Low Hall.

gentlemen who made up the vestry, then governing the parish, and despite a fire in 1791 after a maid's candle set fire to the contents of a linen cupboard, it was quickly rebuilt and back in business. For those at the other end of the social scale there was the Cock, first mentioned in 1747, but very likely to have been a successor to an earlier beerhouse in the vicinity of Mission Grove. There are accounts of fights outside or in the vicinity of the Cock in the 1760s, and in one incident in 1769 after the landlord refused to open up for a group of Irishmen, in which he was struck by a brick during an ensuing riot and fatally injured.

LOW HALL

South of Marsh Street lay open fields and the marshes. Low Hall, roughly on the site of the present Newton Close, existed in 1397 and in 1611 belonged to Richard Garnett, one of several moneyers associated with Walthamstow. In 1822 it still had its ancient moat, and was then a seventeenth-century timber-framed building, brick fronted and with a tiled roof. Latterly it was the home for successive tenant farmers. From 1875 much of the immediate land north of the house was used as Walthamstow's sewage works, though initially the land continued to be farmed. But the filtration processes gradually took over more land until by 1907 only 36 acres remained in agricultural use. Low Hall itself was a war time casualty, being the recipient of a direct hit from a V1 flying bomb in 1944.

Places to pray: church and chapel

THE FIRST CHURCH

Walthamstow's oldest place of worship is St Mary's Church. It had a part to play in the governance of the parish, in its charities, in education and in a host of activities temporal as well as spiritual. There were property rights that affected the church and the clergy, and which shaped the building and the income that sustained it.

There is no certain date ascribed to the first church building on Church Hill. There was a church here prior to 1147, and it is likely that sometime between 1103 and 1130 one of the de Tony family, lords of the manor, gave the church and the income it received from the inhabitants – the tithes – to St Peter of Chatillon by Conches monastery in France. Sometime after the death of Ralph de Tony his widow Alice made a new donation of church, tithes and a little land to Holy Trinity priory at Aldgate, on the request of the rector, Orderic, who had become a monk at the priory. The tithes were later divided between the two houses until the French share was sold to Holy Trinity in 1243. When a vicar was instituted in 1219 the right of his appointment – the advowson – was vested in Holy Trinity priory and this right was retained until the dissolution of the priory in 1532. After that the advowson remained in the hands of the King, and three of Walthamstow's vicars in the critical period of the late Henrican reforms would have been men favoured by Henry VIII or his ministers. It thereafter passed into secular hands, along with the manorial rights that had then become attached to the rectory. The Withypoll family, friends of George Monoux, held them until 1619, when Sir Reginald Argall bought the rights. His brother sold them in 1617 and there followed a protracted dispute between the purchaser, Dr Henry King, archdeacon of Colchester, and the Argall heirs. King won and in turn his heirs sold to the Conyers family in 1689. Eventually the rights were acquired by Edward Warner, finally passing to the Simeon trustees in 1878.

The twelfth-century church of St Mary measured 46' by 24' and would have had a small sanctuary at the east end. All traces above ground have now gone, but it was probably built of flint rubble. The building may have replaced a timber Anglo-Saxon church. In the thirteenth century a

48. St Mary's church and Monoux almshouses. Undated watercolour drawing by Dillon, c.1782. The Monoux chapel roof at the rear of the church is still tiled, and the almshouse has two projecting bays, the nearest of which was removed in the alterations of the late 18th or early 19th century.

49. The Monoux brass in St Mary's church, 1543.

north aisle was added, and a south aisle followed sometime in the fourteenth century. Both aisles extended only as far east as the chancel arch. In the fifteenth century the chancel was extended eastwards and a tower added. There would have been a screen separating the nave and chancel, topped by a rood loft. On the north side of the altar was a statue of St Mary and elsewhere in the church another of St Catherine. Screen, rood loft and statues would all have been destroyed at the time of the Reformation. But there is no record of the exact timings of the upheaval which would have transformed the medieval church with images and possibly relics, into a Protestant place of worship. A stoup, originally intended for holy water, formed part of Monoux's alterations, and still survives in the porch.

George Monoux, who lived through the first stages of the Reformation, funded significant building alterations. In 1535 he repaired the north aisle, and built a chapel on the east end. Pillars replaced the walls of the medieval chancel, and the upper part of the tower, which had required regular repairs, was taken down and replaced by brick, with a circular stairway made to reach the belfry. £1000 from another benefactor, Robert Thorne, a huge sum by sixteenth-century standards, enabled the works to be considerably extended, for also in the same year the south aisle was rebuilt, a porch added and a new chapel built on to it at the east end. During the ensuing century neglect by the Monoux trustees resulted in the areas of the church they had direct responsibility for, the north aisle and Monoux chapel, being often in poor repair. The eighteenth century saw successive wooden galleries built first at the west end, to meet the growing population, but repair work renewed the battlements, and a bequest by Susan Samms in 1715 funded a small cupola on the tower, removed in 1836.

With the church went the glebe land, originally intended to help provide food for the vicar. There were fields near the Lea in Out Mead and near the vicarage. Later enlarged, the bulk of the village glebe land was sold to Essex County Council in 1912 and became the site of the girls' high school.

Ownership rights extended to the church itself. The chancel was the property of the rectors in medieval times. Later vicars claimed it, rights

50. Interior of St Mary's church prior to the removal of the box pews in 1876.

asserted by both Gabriel Grant, the early seventeenth-century vicar, and Edmund Chishull, his early eighteenth-century successor. But in 1730 a new rector reasserted his rights and the control of the chancel remained in the lay rector's hands until sometime in the mid nineteenth century

Responsibility for the repair of the Monoux chapel and the north aisle had been vested in the Marshall family, owners of what had once been Monoux's London properties since 1710, and who also paid the sums due under Monoux's will to the schoolmaster and almspeople. In 1782 Joel Johnson, churchwarden, took the lead in negotiating a new agreement. The effect on the almshouse is detailed in a later chapter, but in exchange for a reduced annual rent charge, the Marshall family relinquished their rights over the church, and the almshouse.

The present appearance of the church owes much to rebuilding work in the nineteenth century. The chancel was raised in 1817-18 and a large east window replaced with a wheel window. Rendering was done in stages, possibly being completed by 1818. Internal alterations in 1876 removed box pews and set back the gallery fronts. The chancel was extended in 1938. The church was bomb damaged in 1940 and gradually restored between 1949 and 1968.

COLOURFUL CLERGYMEN

Walthamstow's Elizabethan, Jacobean and Caroline vicars were a colourful crew. Henry Siddal, vicar from 1557 to 1563, who had been evicted from his previous cure under Mary for being married, was in dispute with the patron, Edmund Withypoll, who refused to recognise him, and evicted him from the vicarage and the glebe lands. Siddal's successor, Richard Pattinson, was driven to prosecute some of his parishioners for non-payment of tithes, and later abandoned the parish. John Reynolds, vicar from 1583 to 1611, was noted as negligent in 1604, while Gabriel Grant's disputes over the ownership of the chancel were overshadowed by a charge of adultery in 1635.

The Elizabethan church settlement was intended to be inclusive, but not all felt the new style of worship was acceptable. The Hale family, which lived at Moons from 1574-1597 remained Catholic, and suffered repeated prosecutions for recusancy. Monoux had had his own private chapel at Moons licensed from 1536 and it is likely that this became a place of secret Catholic worship. Indictments of Catholics continued up to 1629, but in 1676 there were no Catholics in the parish and it was almost another hundred years before another Catholic family, the Bradshaws, are recorded.

51. South-east view of St Mary's church in 1819.

For those wanting reform to go further, there remained the hope that the Elizabethan settlement could be extended. Essex had its share of Puritans, some of whom were to leave for Holland when James I did not introduce Presbyterian forms of worship after his ascent to the throne in 1603. In turn some of these English refugees sailed to America on the Mayflower in 1620. The initial break between King and Parliament in 1642 left Walthamstow in the Parliamentary sphere. There were Royalists like Sir Thomas Merry, but power lay with the Presbyterians. Gabriel Grant had died in 1638, and there followed a period of five years when there was no vicar, Alexander Robinson serving the parish as curate.

In 1643 Parliament abolished the bishops, and the House of Commons Committee appointed Richard Lee as vicar. Lee, who was active in the Solemn League and Covenant, was succeeded by John Dalton in 1646, and Dalton by John Wood a little over a year later. Wood proved highly unpopular with his parishioners and long standing disputes came to a head in 1649, when rioting broke out inside St Mary's Church and 'Very great affronts were offered to the Minister'. The constables were ineffective, by accident or design, and the whole matter came before the Council of State, who considered asking Oliver Cromwell for troops. But there was no recurrence, and on investigation commissioners appointed to enquire into the state of benefices found that Wood was disliked with good reason, and 'is now questioned for his abilities.'

Wood had gone by 1654. His successor, John Piggott, lived at the house later known as the Walnuts next to the churchyard on the north side of Church Lane and not in the vicarage. This building, to the north-west of the church, dated from before 1487. In the mid 1560s it was in poor condition and Gabriel Grant was probably responsible for the sweeping condemnation of it in the 1620s as 'an old rotten house... in times past an alehouse'. It had five or six rooms and a kitchen, milkhouse and buttery. Grant built a cowhouse, stable and hayhouse worth more than the value of the remainder of the property, but by 1643 the whole lot was in a poor state again. The Parliamentary sequestrators had intended it to be repaired, but it was still likely to have been unusable when Piggott died in 1657. His successor was Thomas Cartwright, who had been secretly ordained by one of the ousted Anglican bishops and who was later to become a bishop himself. The entry in the church register alongside the entry for the burial of William Billing on 4 January 1658 suggests that burial services were still taking place in the Puritan fashion, without use of the prayer book: 'This day Will Billing (who was before seduc'd out of ye church by his factious wife) was after their maner rather lay'd in a hole than buried in ye churchyard.' However the inclinations of Cartwright and some of his parishioners lay with the old forms of Anglicanism.

The Restoration of Charles II in 1660 also brought back Anglican worship and the episcopacy, but Walthamstow continued to be unfortunate in its choice of incumbents. As Edmund Chishull later recorded 'In the year 1669 Andrew Casse (then Vicar, but an unhappy and obnoxious person) abdicated the church, and parish, abruptly, upon a Sunday morning, while the congregation were expecting him to perform divine service.' Another long vacancy followed, and it was ten years before Walthamstow got its next vicar.

EARLY NONCONFORMITY

Not all the parishioners were happy with the established church. The Act of Uniformity had enforced the use of the prayer book, and led to the ejection of over 2000 clergy. Among the ejected ministers was Samuel Slater, who lost his living of Bury St Edmunds. By 1672 he was a Walthamstow resident, and when in that year Charles II's Declaration of Indulgence allowed non-Anglican worship, providing that the meeting place was first 'allowed', Slater duly obtained a licence for the first nonconformist meeting place in Walthamstow. The Declaration was rescinded by Act of Parliament in the following year, though Slater stayed on in the parish, presiding over clandestine services until 1675. Walthamstow's meeting would have been supported by wealthy merchants with City connections, just like the contemporary clandestine meetings held in Hackney under the auspices of another ejected minister, William Spurstowe.

Slater's role had been carried on by visiting ministers, but after the flight of James II and the Edict of Toleration of 1690 under William and Mary, meeting houses could be established openly, and one was built on the north side of Marsh Street by William Coward, a wealthy London merchant and Jamaica planter. Coward had moved to a house on Marsh Street a little after 1673, and had probably become Slater's

52. *Samuel Slater.*

patron. He registered his own house for Presbyterian worship in 1716 and in 1718 also registered the Marsh Street meeting house as Independent. The Meeting continued to be served by visiting ministers, among whom were Philip Doddridge and probably the hymn writer and Stoke Newington resident, Isaac Watts. Coward had hoped that Doddridge would establish an academy in Walthamstow to train men for the ministry, as he was already doing at Northampton, but Doddridge declined to move south.

However one of Doddridge's students did come down to Walthamstow for an interview with Coward. Hugh Farmer, then 23 years old, arrived around 8pm in Walthamstow as arranged, but Coward, then in his late eighties, had omitted to tell his guest that his doors were locked at an earlier hour. Farmer could not make anyone in the house hear, but luckily a footman of a neighbour, William Snell, saw him, and Snell invited the young man to stay. The interview was successful, and Farmer was the resident minister until 1780. Coward intended to rebuild the meeting house and demolished it shortly after 1736, but died two years later before the work could be completed. A new house was completed in 1740, and enlarged in 1759 to cater for the growing congregation built up by Farmer.

EDMUND CHISHULL

St Mary's acquired a vicar of distinction at last when Edmund Chishull became the incumbent in 1708. Chishull, born in Bedfordshire in 1671, became chaplain to the English factory at Smyrna on the Turkish coast in 1698, and while there travelled to Ephesus and Constantinople. His return journey in 1702 took him through the Balkans, Hungary and Germany, after which he was the lecturer at St Olave's, Hart Street, before marriage prompted him to look for a benefice. He was chaplain to Queen Anne in 1711 and was also a pluralist, holding the vicarage of Southchurch in Essex, but this did not prevent him being very active in Walthamstow until his death in 1733.

The Great Storm of 1703 had proved too much for the old vicarage, and too much for parish coffers, which only raised enough to fund the repair of part of it. Chishull put his own money into repairs following delays in payments from monies due to one of the parochial charities, the Maynard charity, but in the meantime the state of the unrepaired part was affecting the remainder of the house. Chishull was successful, and in the same year, 1714, also persuaded Francis Eyles, a London alderman living locally, to part with £54 for new velvet coverings for the altar and pulpit, together with a new marble font. The vicar also succeeded in clearing away the old cottages that backed on to the churchyard, but his revival of the dispute over the chancel was more problematic, leading in 1730 to another fight in the church when the rector, one of the Conyers family, and his servants attempted to occupy the rectorial pew by force.

Things quietened down in the later eighteenth century. Parishioners got three services on Sundays and some during the week. However the vicar from 1779 to 1822, Edward Conyers, spent most of his time at Epping, so Walthamstow had to make do with his curates, notably William Sparrow from 1777 to 1816, and the quality of services may have caused some decline in numbers attending. The situation was remedied in 1822, when William Wilson became vicar, serving for the next 26 years. Wilson left the old vicarage to his curates and moved to a house in Grove Road. He was to be active in educational matters, but also recognised that with the gradual

53. William Wilson.

growth in population – rising from 3006 people in 1801 to 4304 in 1821, that St Mary's Church was insufficient to meet the needs of the parish. A chapel of ease, St John's, was built at Chapel End in 1829, and two others followed: St Peter's-in-the-Forest in 1840, and St James' Church in 1842. All three were to become the first daughter parish churches in 1844.

OLD AND NEW MEETINGS

The later eighteenth century saw divisions among the nonconformists. As in Hackney and Stoke Newington, the minister of the Marsh Street meeting house, Joseph Fawcett, leaned towards the new doctrine of Unitarianism. In 1786 the congregation divided over the issue – some remained with Fawcett, but others broke away and established a new meeting house further east on Marsh Street, on a site opposite Palmerston Road. This new Meeting had its own burial ground, shared with the Unitarians in the Old Meeting House, and members inaugurated a day school in 1789, later rebuilt in 1839.

Among later ministers at the New Meeting was George Collison, whose sojourn lasted from 1797 to 1837. He was a tutor at the Hackney Theological Seminary in Well Street and his son was to

54. St John's church.

55. St Peter's church.

56. St James's church.

57. George Collison.

be the principal founder of one of the earliest London commercial cemeteries, Abney Park. During his ministry Collison also served as minister for the Union Chapel, formed in Wood Street in 1807 and meeting in a small room opposite the Duke's Head. Members were also drawn from Anglicans dissatisfied with the lack of preaching at St Mary's Church, and a permanent chapel was established in 1811, near the old Post Office. This was later replaced by a larger lecture hall in 1844. Congregational activities in the area included the foundation of the School for the Daughters of Missionaries, which opened in a house of Marsh Street on the corner with Mission Grove in 1838. After Walthamstow began to develop, the school moved to Sevenoaks in Kent, taking the name Walthamstow Hall in commemoration of its origins.

At the Old Meeting, Fawcett left soon after the split, and the Unitarians had to make do with a series of temporary ministers until 1801, when Eliezar Cogan became minister. Cogan, who lived at Essex Hall, also kept a notable school there, but after his retirement in 1818 the congregation dwindled. The Meeting closed altogether in 1835 and the building was later demolished. The site was taken over for market gardening, until the 1870s, when the New Meeting, in need of a new chapel, found that they were able to acquire the site under the terms of the will of the benefactor, William Coward, and the Marsh Street Congregational Church was built on the site in 1879. In turn the New Meeting was sold to Primitive Methodists and survived until the early 1970s, being finally demolished for redevelopment in 1977.

There were prominent Quaker families – the Westons and the Dilwyns of Higham Hill in the eighteenth century, John Harman of Highams (1797-1835), and in early and mid nineteenth century John Gurney Fry, son of Elizabeth Fry the prison reformer, who lived at Hale End House from 1854-72, and Joseph Gurney, resident at the Limes, Shernhall Street from 1840-1853, though both these families converted to the established church. In adjoining parishes there were Frys, Buxtons, Gurneys and Pellys, all of whom were prominent Friends, but if they met for religious purposes it was in their own homes and no records survive.

John Wesley preached in the open air at Leyton Green, Woodford Green and Woodford Bridge, but not in Walthamstow. Early Methodists may have used the Wood Street congregational chapel in 1810, but there were premises used for Methodist worship at Chapel End from 1816-1819 and another at Wood Street in 1821. In common with other denominations the real growth in congregations and premises belongs to the growth of Walthamstow from the late 1850s and will form part of the chapter charting the transformation from rural parish to outer London suburb.

58. Marsh Street Congregational church.

Parochial people

Having looked around Walthamstow, touched on the hamlets and main houses, and had a breath of religion, it is time to take in a few personalities. Although the chapter heading suggests that our focus will be people encompassed by the parish boundary, it is rarely the case in local history that the people associated with a locality are so bounded. Indeed it is perfectly possible to see the history of an area in terms of a series of movements – of people, or of classes of people – and indeed the history, as distinct from the prehistory, of Walthamstow can be portrayed in just such a way. And as for the period from 1660-1860 it is the middle and upper classes who are better documented, and who began to move out at the end of the period, it is with them that this chapter is mostly concerned.

Walthamstow was a small place, and until the middle of the nineteenth century, the class that was wealthy enough to play a part in local government would have socialised and intermarried. In a parish with little manufacturing industry of any size, they would also have acted as major employers – of servants and those who laboured on the land. The records they left behind give some insight into life in the bigger houses, and these have also been drawn on.

THE CONYERS

Many of the property owners were transient, staying for one or two generations, but there were exceptions. Grosvenor House on Hoe Street *(ill.39)* had its origins in a mansion built about 1600 by Tristram Conyers, a Yorkshireman, who built up an extensive estate in Walthamstow, East Ham, London, Yorkshire and Lincolnshire. Two of his heirs swelled the family fortune from the law and the last of the Conyers, Sir Gerrard Conyers, who died in 1737 aged 88, was a member of the Salters' Company, Governor of the Bank of England and Lord Mayor of London in 1721.

59. Brookfield in Shernhall Street, c.1870. A view from the Houghton album with the Lancaster family on the lawn.

THE COLLARDS

The Collard family association with Walthamstow was even longer than that of the Conyers. Collards are first recorded as yeomen in the northern part of the parish in the fifteenth century, and in 1483 John Collard de Hale bought part of the demesne lands. Jack's House at the Hale *(ill.14)* was their main house, and they gradually built up a holding of 50-60 acres at Hale End, augmented by another 30 acres or so in other parts of the parish, and by short leases of property. Five Collards contributed to the tax of 1534, and seven paid Ship Money tax under Charles I in 1636. From 1684 three generations of Collards supplemented their income from the land by serving as moneyers. The last of the moneyer Collards died in 1791, and being childless, left his estate to his nephew George Collard. George's widowed aunt continued to live in the later family home of Brookfield on Shernhall Street *(ill.59)* until her death in 1842.

George Collard oined East India House in 1796 and also served in the Royal East India Volunteers from 1798, one of a number of such regiments raised in response to the threat from the French. He was promoted to captain in 1805 and retained the title after he had left both the regiment and India House, and on the death of his aunt he and his wife, Jane Sabina, moved into Brookfield. His account book from this time gives an indication of his household expenses for 1842. He made his wife an allowance of £20 per quarter. His household expenses included furniture, twelve glass dessert dishes costing £3 15s 6d, Lapland rugs, a knife basket, a bronzed hall lamp with ball and chain and a mahogany table costing £4. New clothes included gloves, silk handkerchiefs, shoes (£1 7s the pair) and fourteen collars at a shilling each. Other sundries were tooth powder (6d), a comb at 1s 9d (of ivory?), spectacles at 1s 9d and a hair cut at 1s.

Subscriptions and donations, which totalled £21 11s 9d, included such worthy causes as the Kentish Town Clothing Society, the Essex Clergy Benefit Society and local gifts to Spade Husbandry, the National Infants' School and the poor of the Monoux almshouses. Walthamstow's subscription library was not forgotten, nor were the bell ringers, who received 5s.

George Collard was well liked in Walthamstow, and when he died childless in 1853, his funeral procession extended from his house in Shernhall Street right to the doors of St Mary's Church. One feels that the same cannot be said for his wife, who had previously been the widow of Thomas Jones Burton, and in an era in which a married woman had no control over her own property and very limited legal rights, Jane comes over as a formidable character. Her conversion to Catholicism and the dispute with the local Catholic church and her own husband over a donation of land is told later in Victorian Vigour. The Collard family papers also include records of her separation and divorce from her third husband Joseph Philip Shaw dated 1863, at a time when divorce was unusual. Jane, who lived in a house in Hammersmith on her third marriage, had left Shaw in 1861. Claiming cruelty, which was subsequently amended in the final settlement, she was able to retrieve property she alleged her ex-husband had taken from her, including an enamelled brooch with a portrait of George Collard. Perhaps George had a degree of patience which her third husband lacked, but there are hints in the papers that Jane was a difficult personality. In 1860 there was a dispute with a tradesman who had supplied her with four pattern decanters, when she claimed she had ordered three. And in 1861 Mrs Frances Smith, Jane's cook, had to take her former mistress to court to obtain her unpaid wages. There are dark hints that Mrs Smith might have had a drink problem, but her situation was truly desperate, for without a job, without money and without her 'character' – the crucial reference needed to get another situation – she faced the workhouse. This was one case where the courts did not believe Jane and Mrs Smith got her money.

Jane died in October 1862, and was buried with her second husband in St Mary's Church.

JANE BREDELL'S EFFECTS, 1837

George Collard acted as an executor for friends and neighbours, among whom was Miss Jane Bredell of Salters Buildings, who died in 1837. Her furniture, plate and clothes were valued at £287 9s and provide a snap shot of what a prosperous Walthamstow spinster deemed essential for comfortable living.

Among the plate were a coffee pot, 12 antique tea spoons, a small high silver candlestick with snuffers and stand, and two butter boats. The drawing room had a small convex mirror, a mahogany frame sofa with thick hair squab, two bolsters and pillows, while Miss Bredell's library included a bible and prayer book, books on natural history, the works of Pope, 'West's Letters to a Young Lady' and 'Modies Strictures'. The extensive tableware included punch bowls, china dinner plates, octagon blue plates, a tea canister,

60. Rear of Forest Rise. Watercolour by T. Stuart Milner, 1934.

61. Interior of 2 Forest Rise, showing the drawing room and part of hall. Watercolour by Annie R. Hatley, c.1934. Rooms in Jane Bredell's house in nearby Salter's Buildings would not have been dissimilar to this panelled interior.

and cheese and fruit plates and dishes.

Much of the furniture was mahogany, including a three-drawer dressing chest, a portable desk and 'nail over' chairs, although there were some more exotic items, including a japanned India dressing box, with small boxes inside and an Indian Palimpore. There are few carpets and curtains listed – one Kidderminster carpet in the back room and a pair of scarlet cloth curtains on the ground floor. Miss Bredell's jewellery included three rows of stock pearls, a black and white necklace, jet and diamond earrings, a gold filigree smelling bottle, several rings (diamond and mourning rings) and a pair of opera glasses and their case.

Her wardrobe included a white silk bonnet, a swansdown hat and tippet, and selection of petticoats – made of flannel for the upper and dimity for the under petticoats. There was but one pair of stays. There were cotton and black silk stockings, and decorations included two ostrich feathers, black veils and some Brussels lace. There was also a range of gowns – white, silk and merino and old black and muslin ones. Accessories included five shawls, two silk and velvet bags and an umbrella.

62. The family of William A. Longmore, architect and surveyor, taken at the rear of their house, Brighton Villa, on the north side of Prospect Hill, about 1878. Longmore worked for Walthamstow School Board from 1880. His eldest son, also William, had left home when this view was taken. Behind his wife Maria is his eldest daughter Laura (b.1860) and the group also includes Herbert (b.1864), Felix (b.1868) and Dora, the baby (b.c.1876.)

ROBERT WIGRAM AND 23 CHILDREN

Although there were well established local families, the proximity to London made Walthamstow a suitable place for a man with City connections to have a country house. One such was Robert Wigram (1744-1830), born in Wexford and the son of a sea captain whom he never met for his father was away at sea in a ship that was lost. Brought up by his uncle and mother, Robert came to London in 1762 with £200, trained as a surgeon, and between 1764 and 1770 served as a ship's surgeon on three of the East India Company's vessels travelling to India and China. On his first voyage he met William Money, who was to be a friend and from 1790 a neighbour at Wood End House on Wood Street. An attack of ophthalmia forced him to change profession, and he turned to trade, working as a general merchant, but later to expand into brewing, shipbuilding and a host of associated activities.

In 1772 Wigram married Catherine Brodhurst, who was from a Unitarian family. Besides a London house in Union Court, they had a small house in Wood Street, Walthamstow. By 1780, he had moved to Clay Street, where he and a neighbour Joel Johnson witnessed the fires rising from the City during the Gordon Riots. By 1782 Robert had moved his town residence to the substantial no. 4 Crosby Square, which also served as his place of business, and used his expanded income to buy Walthamstow House at the north end of Shernhall Street, which he had rebuilt and enlarged. The death of Catherine Wigram in 1786 prompted him to let Walthamstow House and move to Knotts Green in Leyton for a while, but he finally prevailed upon Eleanor Watts after three attempts, and they married in 1787. To the six children of his first marriage, he and Eleanor added a further seventeen. Remarkably only one died in infancy. The first son of the second marriage was named after Captain Money, who repaid the compliment with one of his own sons, so that the parish boasted a Money Wigram and a Wigram Money. Robert's mother-in-law also came to live with the family. Mrs Watts kept her money sewn up in her stays and had no hesitation in delving for it whoever was present.

In 1788 Robert bought a ship from his friend William Money, and this was the foundation of a substantial shipping concern, one of which, a 30-gun ship with a crew of 100, built in 1799, was named Walthamstow. On her maiden voyage the commander was William Taylor Money, son of William Money. Robert also bought into Reid's

Brewery and Huddart's Ropeworks, becoming chairman of both concerns, as well as chairman of the East India Docks and principal of Blackwall Shipbuilding Yard. He became the Member of Parliament for Fowey in Cornwall in 1802. There is a story that a judicious 'good night' to Prime Minister William Pitt the Younger immediately after a defeat in the House was rewarded with a baronetcy – but whatever the cause, Wigram was so honoured in 1805, switching to become MP for his home town of Wexford in the following year. He left the Commons in 1817.

From 1819 Sir Robert began to wind down his business affairs, retiring from the Blackwall Yard and passing control of the brewery and the yard to his sons. A letter written from Walthamstow House to his wife in the following year gives some flavour of the size of his establishment – and the domestic concerns of a rich man advising his wife on how she should expect to live after his death:

> "You should give up your Chariot and be content with the Coach, one coachman, three coach horses with a saddle horse for yourself, this will fill the Coach Stable etc if you keep the seven stall stable for 2 or 3 ponies and your Sons that live with you; leave the other Stables and Coach Houses for our family children etc... Hay free but corn and straw some years would come to so large a sum that you must get your Sons to manage that for you and pay for corn and straw amongst themselves. A Groom to manage with your Coachman and one farm Man such as your present Cow Man will do all that will be wanted, as keeping two cows that are in milk and changing them as they get dry for two more, will answer. Pigs and poultry, except for one Sow fed by wash and vegetables etc and a few hens for eggs will be all that is necessary
>
> I do not think a Carter and team is necessary, one old Coach Horse for a single cart the gardener will want and you must pay for carting your Hay and Coals as Mr Reed and C.Bellamy does.
>
> One servant out of livery and one in livery, with your groom on occasion may answer as the Groom or the Young Man who chance to live with you must assist in the House when you have Company; every Young Man must pay for his own washing.
>
> The female Establishment in the House now will bear cutting down, but I confess myself ignorant how to do it, you must therefore exercise your own judgement. A Cook and Housekeeper and Lady Maid will be a great saving. The consumption of Porter in this House is beyond bounds, it should be brought down to a Barrel a fortnight (I shall not be then a Brewer) or 26 barrels a year at the most.
>
> The Expenses of Education, Clothing etc of each child must be deducted from the interest of his or her Fortune.
>
> All the Tradesmen's Bills must be kept down by ordering them in writing not to do anything without your positive direction.
>
> One heavy expense, the washing must be made directly by the Young Men putting out all their washing... "

At least two servants would have been exempted from any scaling down of the household. Ann Pearce had been taken on by Robert Wigram in 1772 and nursed all 23 of his children. During her 48 years of service she was said to have become something of an autocrat; certainly she was important enough to be painted before her death at Walthamstow House in 1822. Nanny Pearce had her City counterpart in Alice Escott, who had put in 41 years of service as housekeeper at no. 3 Crosby Square at the time of her death in 1837.

63. Ann 'Nanny' Pearce. The family remembered her as something of an autocrat! Watercolour by M. de la Coeur.

64. Robert Fitz-Wygram. Painting by T. Phillips, 1837. From an engraving by Joseph Brown.

Wigram died in 1830. His heir became Sir Robert Fitz-wygram who let Walthamstow House after the death of his stepmother in 1841. The house became a school and then an orphanage – Walthamstow of the 1860s was ceasing to be a place for a country retreat, and what had been convenient for the ennobled City man was not suitable for his heir.

JOEL JOHNSON

A man of much humbler beginnings was Joel Johnson, who in later life produced a chronological summary of his life and origins. His father had been a bricklayer's apprentice in Croydon in 1722, but rose to become a surveyor to the Hand in Hand Fire Office. Johnson was born in 1720 in Vere Street, near Oxford Street. His father died when he was 11, but he was able to train as a builder. His association with Walthamstow began in 1759 when he took lodging in a house in Marsh Street. His second wife died in the same year and he set up as an architect, taking a Mr Langley, a carpenter, into partnership. Langley became his son-in-law in 1764.

Johnson also tried his hand at inventions and designed a lock to make the mails at the General Post Office more secure, for which he received a £200 reward. He married again in 1771; his bride, Sarah Parker, was a widow of a Dedham man and had a four-year-old son. In addition to raising a family, and commissions that included work for Bond Hopkins at Clapham and Hackney, Johnson, a nonconformist, was also chosen to be churchwarden in 1778 and served for six successive years. He provided uniforms for the Monoux children, partially from his own pocket, and also helped with uniforms for the nonconformist Green School when that was founded in 1789. This led to questions being asked by his fellow trustees as to whether Anglican Blue School money would be used to help the nonconformist Green School. Johnson was asked to meet his fellow trustees after morning service, but he declined, pointing out that he was now so deaf that it would be little use his coming. The remaining trustees pressed for a meeting for the following Sunday and Johnson duly attended, but felt so angry that his probity was being questioned that he handed over the unpaid school accounts and gave up his management.

Johnson had taken a house in Clay Street, from where he had two of his children inoculated against smallpox in 1780. In June of the same year the anti-Catholic Gordon riots broke out in London, and like his neighbour Robert Wigram, Johnson was a witness to the effects of a breakdown in law and order that seemed very threatening. His house was situated:

> ... as to enable us to see from the windows great numbers of Church Steeples and Spires when the mob fired the prisons and buildings in the night, we with tears in our eyes for the distress of others, and knowing but our nearest friends were the sufferers or perhaps our own property destroying, while we counted fourteen large fires, besides smaller ones blazing at once, partly knowing by the spires where they were, though not what they were.

Johnson's buildings included the church of St John at Wapping (1756), Magdalen Hospital, St George's in the Fields and part of the Royal London Hospital. He was a warden of the Carpenters' Company and Master in 1789. After the dispute with his fellow parishioners, he moved to his wife's former parish of Dedham to manage a factory and died aged 78 in 1799. He is buried in St Mary's churchyard at Walthamstow.

65. William Houghton and his youngest son Edmund. Edmund was aged eight in 1871 and this view dates from around that period.

WILLIAM HOUGHTON

Forty years later, Walthamstow was still a place to attract the up and coming man from the City. William Houghton was born in Wickham, Hampshire in 1819. He came to London to be articled to a Mr Badham, a solicitor practising in the City, and rose to become a partner in the firm and then to take on the whole concern on Badham's retirement. He first came to Walthamstow in 1838, and on his marriage around 1848 took a tall house on the east side of Wood Street, with a view over Turner and Budd's stable yard and over the road from Wood End House. Houghton also built up a local practice and benefited greatly from a variety of local government work.

In 1871 he, his wife Emma and five of their six children still lived in the Wood Street house. Gilbert Houghton recalled the house as none too convenient. The water supply came from a well in the garden, with a pump in the scullery. Hot water came from the kitchen fire or from a kettle over the fire. There was no bathroom so servants provided a hip bath in each bedroom, with cans of hot and cold water for the weekly bath. Lighting was by composite candles in the parlour and tallow dips for the rest of the house. Later in the century lighting would have been improved by

66. Frederick (b.1860) and Edmund Houghton outside the coach house of the Red House in the late 1870s.

oil lamps to supplement the candles, but even then one woman remembered winter evenings in an old Hoe Street house when she was a girl and had to walk down long dark passages of flickering shadows, and of a black piece of staircase which had to be crossed before the welcoming line of light of the nursery door proclaimed safety. The Houghton's house cannot have been too different for their children.

Gilbert does not recall the servants, but in 1871 the household had three resident servants – two described as 'domestic' and one cook. Additionally there was a gardener, Benjamin Warwick, aged 64, who lived in Baker's Arms Yard off Chestnut Avenue. He may have been trained as a gardener in one of the big local houses, and may have worked for more than one local family.

William moved his family to the Red House, Hoe Street in the following year, which had more space and larger grounds. Some of the family photographs, now saved in the Houghton album at Vestry House Museum, are taken there, either in the garden or in the stable yard.

67. Benjamin Warwick, the Houghtons' gardener, c.1870.

JOHN HARMAN AND THE RED BOOK OF HIGHAMS

Pleasure grounds and gardens would have been one of the advantages enjoyed by the City man escaping the narrow courts for the near country retreat of Walthamstow up to the mid nineteenth century. In 1790 the banker John Harman bought the manor of Higham Bensted and with it the new manor house *(ill.20)*. This had been built in 1768 to the design of William Newton and originally consisted of a five-bay central block of two storeys, with gigantic pilasters on the east front, flanked by single-storey pedimented wings. To the west the ground fell away sharply, revealing part of the basement. The previous owner, William Hornby, had removed the pediment in the central block and added a balustraded third storey and a central cupola between 1785 and 1790.

In 1793 John Harman called in an expert, Humphry Repton, who had built up a distinguished client list for architectural alterations and landscaping estates to provide sweeping vistas in the best Romantic style. He produced a short essay for each client, with plans and drawings, bound up in red leather, from which they take their name of Red Books. To illustrate how he proposed to make improvements, his watercolours had added flaps, which could be pulled across to cover features marked for removal. Repton visited Higham Hill, as the house was known, on 24 November 1793. He found that Hornby's alterations had made the house too high for its breadth and designed a continuous iron balcony for the west front at ground floor

68. Section of boathouse at Highams. Watercolour by Humphry Repton in the Red Book of Highams.

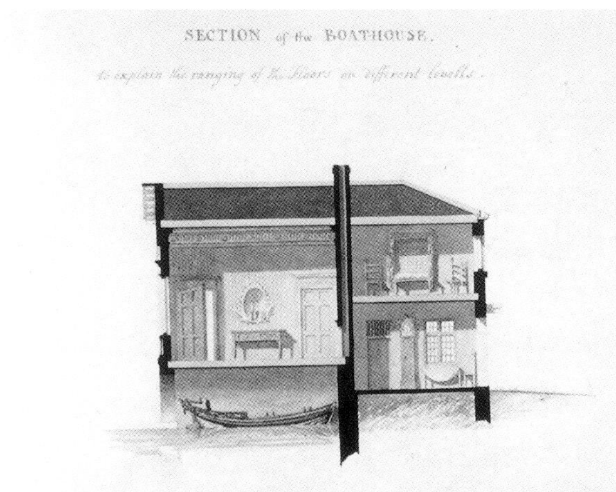

69. *Front of the boat house from Highams Lake. Watercolour by Humphry Repton in the Red Book of Highams.*

70. *Higham Hill from the park, before improvements. The kitchen garden was to be removed and the front of the house altered. Watercolour by Humphry Repton in the Red Book of Highams.*

level, supported by stucco arches which formed an arcade over the basement windows. The intention was also 'to prevent that degree of horror which always accompanies a view from a precipice'. The kitchen garden was to be removed to the south-east side and the view of 'the naked village' planted out. The view was to be improved so that lawn and park appeared to belong to the house, with the addition of a Doric seat and a new lake. Repton proposed to build a two-storey cottage over the dam at the south end, which would also act as a boat house and a lodge, with a withdrawing room for ladies or as a vestibule for the larger room with views out over the lake. Waste water would be used to power an occasional cascade, with the option of having it in use only when the cottage was in use. Although Repton did not recommend that the estate be approached from this side, the cottage could also serve as a lodge to allow the family a summer approach road.

John Harman had the lake constructed and the house altered, and many of Repton's alterations to the park were implemented. It is likely that Edward Warner made later changes to the estate when he acquired it in 1849, including two additional bays to the south end of the west front, with a matching extension to Repton's balcony, and raising the ground level on the centre of the east front. In turn this allowed the steps to be removed and a porch to be added. The roof cupola had already been replaced by a wider lantern tower. Later alterations to the house were made after it was taken over to become Woodford county high school for girls in 1919.

CHIMNEYS SWEPT

Besides their gardeners and live-in servants, the larger houses would have needed the services of specialists. All were heated by coal, and their chimneys, often tall and narrow, had to be cleaned by hand. There were no extendable brushes, and chimney sweeps would employ boys to scale the inside of the chimneys. In 1808 one such boy was working at a house on the High Street near the present junction with Pretoria Avenue belonging

71. Higham Hill in 1820. Watercolour by John Varley. Undated but likely to be c.1820. The women may be members of John Harman's family.

to a Mr Jeffreys, a carpenter. On his way down he got stuck in the flue. Luckily Mrs Jeffrey was nearby and heard his cries for help. The chimney pot and several rows of bricks were removed and the unfortunate lad extracted in ten minutes – before he was overcome by the fumes. The sweep arrived on the scene shortly afterwards, and blaming the weakened child for the accident, hit him, before sending him off to sweep another chimney. Onlookers discovered that the boy had been working since 3am and had travelled to and from Wanstead before his accident.

This case and others like it were used by campaigners who eventually abolished the employment of child sweeps. Walthamstow had a positive contribution to make to the campaign, since it was a local resident who invented the folding flexible chimney brush.

SELECTED FAMOUS

Among our parochial people were a number famous in their day. John Stanley (1714-86), composer and musician, who was also blind, lived at Salter's Buildings. William Morris (1834-96) was born at Elm House on Clay Street and lived there for the first six years of his life. His father had taken the house in 1833, and like William Houghton travelled into the City by Wragg's stage coach, and when business prospered he was able to move further out, taking Woodford Hall. After his death in 1847 his widow moved the family back to Walthamstow, renting Water House from 1848 to 1856. Water House was then bought by the newspaper proprietor Edward Lloyd, whose name is commemorated in the park created from the grounds of Water House, which now houses the William Morris Gallery. Morris' socialist principles were to make him an important figure for twentieth-century Walthamstow, and his writings were to provide the motto for the new borough in 1929.

72. William Morris.

MIGRANTS AND REFUGEES

Walthamstow was host to two unusual groups of temporary immigrants in the 1830s. In 1826 *HMS Beagle* was sent off on a voyage of scientific exploration of the tip of South America, and on her return to England in 1830, the captain had on board four natives of Tierra del Fuego, two men, a girl of nine and an adolescent of fourteen, whom he had named *Boat Memory, York Minster, Fuegia Basket* and *Jimmy Button*. Boat Memory, thought to be the brightest of the group, died of smallpox in Plymouth on arrival, but the other three were vaccinated and at the captain's expense sent to lodge with the vicar of Walthamstow, William Wilson, at his house in Grove Road. Wilson' s school taught them English and Christianity, as well as some practical skills of carpentry and gardening. It was intended that the three should be used to spearhead the introduction of European ways to their compatriots on their return to Tierra del Fuego.

The three Fuegians were presented to King William IV and Queen Adelaide at St James' Palace some nine months after their arrival, and spent a year in total in Walthamstow before returning to Tierra del Fuego on the *Beagle* in December 1831, in the company of a young missionary called Richard Matthews, who had been recommended by William Wilson. The party arrived in January 1833, and Jimmy Button was reunited with his family – though little emotion was displayed on either side. Fuegia Basket and York Minister were married by Matthews, who was left with the natives while the *Beagle* went off on a short voyage of exploration. On returning the crew found that much of the goods left behind had been stolen, and Button had been robbed by his two former companions. Matthews was taken off by the crew.

73. Grove House.

The three Fuegian travellers soon shed all elements of the crash course in nineteenth-century English culture. York Minster was later killed in a feud. Button led a massacre of eight missionaries in 1859, though a son of his also made a trip to England in 1866. Fuegia Basket was last seen by an Englishman in 1883, who recorded that she was dying, aged only 44.

It was missionary activity that was responsible for the visit of a group of Malagasy to Walthamstow in 1839, this time as refugees – asylum seekers in present-day parlance. Early support in Madagascar from the royal family for Christianity from 1818 onwards had been reversed in 1835. One princess who had become a convert, Rafarvavy, was sentenced to death, and although reprieved was sold into slavery. She escaped, and with a group of six other Malagasy Christians got to Mauritius. Rafarvavy and five of her companions were then sent on to England and stayed in Walthamstow as guests of the New Meeting. Her four male companions stayed with the master of the British school and all attended the newly open British school. Sadly Rafarvavy was not strong enough after the suffering she had endured to survive the rigours of a Walthamstow winter, and died on 26 December 1840. She was buried in the New Meeting burial ground, a poignant link between alien cultures.

GIPSY SMITH

Almost by definition, gipsies cannot be parochial people, constantly crossing settled boundaries and regarded with a mixture of fascination and persecution. On 31 March 1860 Cornelius and Mary Smith's caravan had rested on Upper Mill Plain in Epping Forest, within Walthamstow parish. There, under a hornbeam tree, Mary gave birth to her fourth child and second son, Rodney Smith. As 'Gipsy Smith' he was to become a great evangelist, working with William Booth's Salvation Army and travelling extensively in his missionary activity. He died in 1947 on the ocean liner the *Queen Mary*, bound for the USA. His ashes were brought back to England by his second wife and buried beneath his birth tree. A small granite monument marks the spot, put up in 1949.

Rate and regulate: parish government

Four groups of people exercised degrees of control over local people's lives from the late medieval period. The manorial courts regulated land tenure and use and other daily functions, including cleansing of ditches and the quality of local ale. Royal officials regulated the Forest, although their powers were in decline from the mid seventeenth century. Quarter sessions held powers over roads and bridges, and justices of the peace, increasingly charged with implementing 'stacks of statutes', dealt with issues of law and order, regulation of the poor law, and local taxation. Lastly there was the church, with the regulation of moral life, administration of local charitable bequests and maintenance of the parish church. The parish gradually built up its own range of local functions, enhanced by Elizabethan legislation on highways (1555) and a range of acts on parochial responsibility for the poor, culminating in the Poor Law Act of 1601. The influence of the manors in local government gradually waned through the seventeenth century, but did not wholly disappear, while the royal regulation of the Forest also weakened. Both have been considered in earlier chapters and this and the next chapter are concerned with parochial affairs and the regulation of law and order.

THE VESTRY

The parish governed its affairs through the vestry, which began as an open meeting of inhabitants in a room at the church. Men were chosen for the honorary offices – a surveyor of the highways responsible for the upkeep of local roads and for the contribution of the inhabitants towards statutory labour, one or two churchwardens, whose responsibilities included local charities, the church fabric and a range of other duties, and one or more overseers of the poor. All three sets of office holders would have to lay out their own money in local costs which could then be recovered from the parish, and in turn the parish would levy local rates to meet these expenses.

Vestries could be open to all, but in Walthamstow the vicar, Gabriel Grant, a churchwarden and some of the inhabitants petitioned the Bishop of London for a select vestry, claiming it would avoid disorder at meetings. Their petition was granted, with the effect that the vestry could choose its own membership. No records survive for the period of the select vestry, which was probably dissolved by Edmund Chishull, when he became vicar in 1708. Certainly when the surviving vestry minutes begin in 1710 it was open again.

In the eighteenth century there were two regular meetings, one in Easter week and the other in September or December, but the vestry also met when required. Before 1730 it usually met at St Mary's Church, but afterwards in the vestry room in the workhouse. Longer meetings were adjourned to the Chequers public house on Marsh Street or the Nag's Head opposite the church – like the manorial courts, vestry meetings could also be partly social occasions. Until the early 1780s the average attendance was ten people, but as business and population grew attendances rose, the highest being 116 people for the election of a beadle in 1805. More complex business was delegated to ad hoc committees.

PARISH OFFICIALS

Office holding was not popular as it took time away from business which might well be based in the City. People paid fines to be exempted or paid for substitutes, sometimes of variable quality. Before 1766 the two elected surveyors divided their duties between the marsh or lower division and the forest or upper division; after that date the parish employed a surveyor until 1825 when the position became elective again.

There were other paid officials. The parish clerk had received a pension under the terms of George Monoux's will of 1544, but from 1749 a salaried clerk was also employed. The duties of this post rapidly grew and by the time of Richard Banks' appointment in 1779, the clerk made up rate books, and collected parish rates and rents. From 1739 a beadle was employed to deal with parish vagrants and was given his own uniform and staff from 1742. Sadly the staff, which was loaned to Vestry House Museum, was stolen. The beadle or workhouse master also acted as an assistant overseer, but this became a full-time paid post from 1820.

There were irregular appointments of parish constables. Besides the poor and the church, the other main expenses were the digging, carting and carriage of gravel for the parish roads. Road work was even more unpopular, and there were frequent presentations at quarter sessions of those who tried to avoid their statutory duties between 1601 and 1662. By the mid eighteenth century money was being sought from carriage owners in the parish and it is probable that monetary payments were gradually replacing statutory labour, although in 1780 the assistant overseer was urged to employ the able bodied poor on the roads where possible. The parish also had its own fire engine, presented by Ralph Fressleicque in 1771. It was replaced in 1791 and repaired at parish expense, coming under the parish's police sergeant, who acted as engine keeper in 1836.

PERAMBULATION

In 1801 Walthamstow had a total population of 3006. Parish administration was an affair between neighbours and as with the enactment of manorial business, the social element was important. Memory was by association before there were documents, and in one aspect of parish life this persisted. Before there were maps, the boundaries of the parish had to be remembered and checked to make sure that there had been no encroachment by neighbouring parishes. Traditionally this was done by a mixture of young and old. By the eighteenth century perambulations were sometimes written down and records survive of Walthamstow walks in 1780, 1816 and 1830. In 1780 warnings were issued in advance to property owners whose buildings, ponds and walls straddled the boundary to provide the means of crossing obstructions. About eighty horsemen and as many on foot met at the Church at 8am on Ascension Day and set off to the sound of church bells, and fife and drum borrowed from a unity of the Derby militia, then based at Tottenham and Edmonton. The leaders were also equipped with planks to cross small streams and ditches, a perambulator – an instrument to enable them to measure the bends of the River Lea. Bread, cheese and ale had been ordered up in advance – supplies at the Ferry House being paid for by the lord of the manor of Salisbury Hall. By boundary marks boys were bumped to ensure that they would remember the place for the next occasion. There was foolery with the boats and some fancy riding, not all of which had quite the intended effect, as John Dench of the Duke's Head,

74. The Horse and Groom, which straddled the Walthamstow and Leyton boundary, from the western side of the river. Watercolour by C. Bigot c.1820.

Wood Street discovered – 'in leaping over one place came down in the Mud, Horse and all, but luckily received no hurts, but made a little sport and laughter for the rest of the Company'. The perambulation finished at 6 o'clock with a march down Wood Street, behind the church, and down Marsh Street to Hillyers ferry to a substantial dinner.

Folk whose property straddled the border could view the proceedings with mixed feelings. In May 1830 a Walthamstow party walked the Slip, the detached piece of land which lay parallel to and south of the main border within Leyton parish. Down by the mill at Lea Bridge they walked through the cellar of a pub called the Horse and Groom, through the tap room and out the other side, although naturally there was a break for refreshment ...

> 'and as the number of persons was considerable they gave full occupation to the people of the house, which seemed to excite a smile of satisfaction upon the countenance of the Landlord. While thus employed in the course of conversation it was suggested by Mr Humphreys the late churchwarden that the Horse and Groom or part of the house being situated in the Parish of Walthamstow, should contribute something towards the rates of the parish and might accordingly be assessed in a small sum, say one or two guineas per annum. Upon the hearing of this unwelcome intelligence, the hilarity of the host was suddenly converted into gloom and the change which took place in his countenance was very sudden and very amusing.'

Presumably the party had finished their bread and ale before this tactless announcement.

CHARITIES

Much of the serious business of the parish was concerned with the poor – through the administration of parochial charities and the poor law itself. Before the Reformation alms were given for the remission of the soul from Purgatory, and could include payments for the saying of prayers for the departed donor. William Hyll, vicar of Walthamstow from 1470-87, was the earliest recorded Walthamstow benefactor, leaving an acre of meadow to the parish in his will of 1487 on condition that his anniversary and that of his parents was remembered. After 1826 the annual income of £2. 5s was paid into the general charities account, and the parish continued to own the acre until 1938.

GEORGE MONOUX

There were elements of commemoration in the benefaction of Walthamstow's most famous gift, but George Monoux was more ambitious in his generosity. Monoux built up a fortune as a merchant adventurer in Bristol in the 1480s and moved to London early in the new century, where he turned to the cloth trade. He became a member of the Drapers' Company, serving as warden, and having six stints as master between 1508 and 1540. As befitted his status in the guild, he also served as a City alderman from 1507, with a period from 1509-10 as sheriff, and 1514-15 as lord mayor. In 1523 he was also MP for the City, though he declined a second term as mayor on grounds of ill health. His London house was in Crooked Lane, near the church of St Lawrence Pountney, and he built up extensive land holdings in the City of London, Bedfordshire, Essex, Norfolk, Yorkshire and six other counties. His Walthamstow association began in 1507 with the acquisition of a house and land on Billet Lane later known as Moons, a name arising from the local pronunciation of Monoux. This formed a country seat close enough to the City for relatively easy travel, though not that easy, since among Monoux's benefactions was the repair of the wooden causeway over the marshes to the Lock Bridge (near the present bridge on Lea Bridge Road).

As a member of the Drapers' Company, Monoux would have been part of a social group that gave to charity, and the City livery companies later came to administer many bequests made by members. Monoux determined to do something for the Walthamstow poor. In 1527 his steward Richard Vaughan 'entered peasibly into a certain parcelle of ground lymited and set out on the north parte of the Church yarde', an acquisition witnessed by Monoux's fellow Bristol merchant Paul Withypoll, whose brother Richard was to acquire the rights to appoint the vicar of St Mary's Church in 1534. Monoux intended to build a school and almshouse on the land and drew up his own specification. The almshouse was to have thirteen rooms, each measuring thirteen feet by seventeen feet, with windows and doors front and back, and a shared chimney and their own back yard. In the centre of the range would be a four-room schoolmaster's house on two floors. Two external staircases would reach up to two upper rooms, one for the school and the other to serve as a church house. In later documents, Monoux made it clear that he intended these

75. Monoux almshouses.

rooms to be used for parish dinners, dinners for his future trustees and wedding feasts for poor people. An additional property to the north of the almshouse range, also owned by Monoux, was fitted out with 'great Spitts, Andirons, Pewter and other necessaries for the dressing of said Dinner'. Later this house was linked directly to the first floor of the almshouse range by a set of stairs.

Monoux also drew up rules for the running of the almshouse after construction had been completed in 1541. The almspriest and schoolmaster, who was to be of quiet and honest conversation, was to pray for the souls of George Monoux and his family. His wages of £6 13s 4d per year were supplemented by a gift of 6s 8d and he was also expected to teach up to thirty children of the parish. His accommodation was free, but he was not to absent himself for more than two days without licence. He was to regularly ensure the almsfolk knew the rules of the establishment and that they received their weekly 7d and their share in the £5 annual free coal in winter.

The eight almsfolk had to demonstrate their ability to pray, attend mass daily, not fight or brawl, pray for the founder and his family and not throw rubbish into the churchyard. Breaking any man's hedge or woods was also forbidden 'or if any of them do frequent or sit drinking in any alehouse, and having been by my executors warned of the same on two occasions, then at the third time of offending they shall be exiled from the almshouse and the benefit therof forever'. In other words, stay away from the Nag's Head, then on the other side of the churchyard! In a compassionate clause compared to other almshouse charities, the death of a husband or wife did not mean that the survivor lost his or her place – unless they married again.

Monoux's will dated 6 June 1541 assigned property in the City parish of All Hallows Staining to meet the expenses of the charity, including £42 17s 4d for running costs and £1 6s 8d to the parish clerk to help with teaching. In the event of his heirs failing in their duties, these were to revert to the Mayor and Commonality of the City of London. Monoux died in 1544 and for a while his charity ran smoothly. But his heir William Monoux died childless in 1549, and by 1561 only Richard Vaughan remained of the original trustees. Vaughan appropriated the house to the north of the almshouses for his own use, pulled down part of the almshouse and tried to convert the remainder into a stable. George Monoux junior, William's brother, eventually evicted Vaughan and regained control of the property. An inquisition on the charity held in 1636 recorded

> And that the said Richard Vaughan, before his death, was much troubled in his mind, hateing the sight of all manner of light by Sunn, Monne, Candle or ffire fore that he would not see the Devill fetch him away alive, and afterwards dyed miserably.

Which may have been of some comfort to any evicted almsfolk.

In 1563 George Monoux junior vested the almshouses and their supporting London property into the hands of Edward Alford, son of one of the original trustees. However Edward and his son John proved to be little better, as the inquisition of 1636 found. The almshouses were in poor repair, the stipends had been paid irregularly, and when one vicar had suggested they fund an annual sermon in memory of George Monoux the Alfords refused. The schoolmasters had been of variable quality, some having no grasp of Latin, and the Alfords had filled the almshouses with people from places other than Walthamstow, sometimes in response to bribes, notably in the 1600s 'a Lunaticke person and dangerous and fearefull to divers of the Inhabitants of the said parish'. Walthamstow parishioners had had to meet the cost of the local poor and the almshouse folk from their own pockets. In 1599 Elizabeth Alford, Edward's mother, vested a rent charge of £9 for the benefit of the almsfolk, and this was conveyed to the charity trustees by her son in 1599, but this bequest was also poorly managed.

An attempt by the Corporation of London to oust the Alfords in 1635 eventually failed in the courts in 1637 and the Alfords held on. The value of the Monoux property had risen to over £600 per year by the 1650s and Walthamstow parish made two attempts to have the almsfolk's stipends increased. In 1659 the parish obtained a ruling from a commission in their favour, but it was not acted on. Building repairs made around 1700 were probably the result of a bequest of Henry Maynard. The eastern end was almost wholly rebuilt in the late eighteenth century, but the western end retained its original small Tudor red bricks until it was destroyed by a German bomb in 1940.

There were later bequests which made provision for the Monoux almshouses – from Richard Banks in 1812, from John Harman of Highams in 1817, from William Bedford in 1822 and Elizabeth Collard in 1842. There were also a number of other bequests for general relief of poverty. Robert Rampston left £2 a year for the poor, which the churchwardens distributed in the form of bread in 1796. One of the alms priests, Thomas Colby, who died in 1609, left all his estate in trust for the poor, although his trustees did not comply with his wishes, and it took an inquisition of 1633 to recover £120 for the parish, which was then invested in twelve acres of land at Hale End called Hellbrinkes or Hale Brinks. Rent charges on local property provided the income for the bequests of Richard Garnett (1623) and Thomas Gamuel (1643), while a group of local people came together anonymously to contribute £95 for the purchase of land in 1650. The income from the Inhabitants Donation subsequently came from a field south of Haggar Lane, later the site of Hempstead, Fyfield and Forest roads, and Fernhilll Court.

Henry Maynard's bequest was more substantial, as he left £950 in his will of 1686 to buy land to support the minister, the schoolmaster and the poor, and provide small annual gifts to the parish clerk, churchwardens and overseers. Maynard's executor bought Higham Hill Farm, but a legal dispute delayed the establishment of the charity and once this was settled, arrears of income were used to buy Stretman's Farm of thirty acres at Hale End.

SQUIRE'S ALMSHOUSES

Walthamstow gained another set of almshouses in 1795, when Mary Squire paid for the construction of six almshouses on the west side of the churchyard 'for the widows of decayed tradesmen' who also had to be Anglicans. The site was a gift from John Conyers, and Mary Squire's investment of £1000 of stock provided money for maintenance and an annual pension of £5 for each almswoman.

By 1786 there was a total of sixteen dole charities, yielding an annual income of £258. In the early nineteenth century some of the funds went

76. Squire's almshouses in 2001.

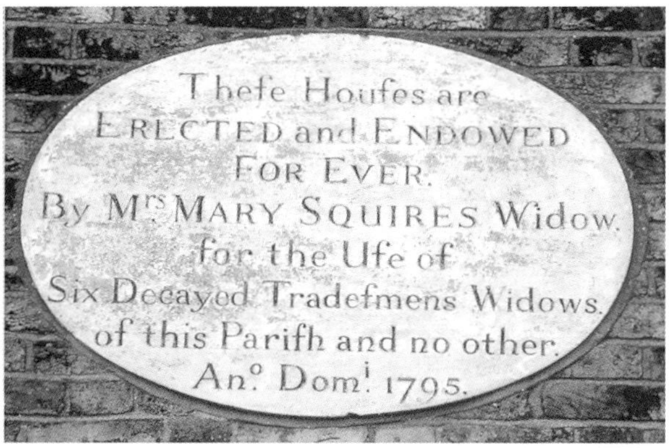

77. Plaque on Squire's almshouses.

into the churchwarden's general account, a loss to the poor made worse in 1825 when the parish collector embezzled £150. By 1831 the total charitable income was £850 per year.

The combined income from these charities enabled the parish to fund pension relief to some of the poorest inhabitants. In 1710 the overseers' records include monthly payments to twenty people of sums ranging from 4s to 12s. There were also incidental expenses – after a drowning in the Lea, charges to apprentice poor children, doctors' bills and payments for clothing. These included money to allow the redemption of pawned items, though it was Leyton parish in the 1740s which paid Beck Mitten 'to git her stays out of pawn'. In 1710 Walthamstow raised two sets of church rates for 3d in the pound, but in effect charity income, and notably charity income that had been intended for specific purposes, was being used to meet the cost of the poor, and keep the rates down. The next chapter examines how the rising cost of the poor law was dealt with in the eighteenth century.

'Neither should he eat' : the problem of the poor

THE POOR LAWS

It was Elizabethan legislation that defined the role of the parish in coping with the poor. From 1563 householders had to contribute to the cost of poor relief. In 1572 justices of the peace had to register the aged and impotent who had been resident in each division of a county for three years and then assess and tax the inhabitants for the costs of poor relief. In 1576 parishes were to provide work for the poor. Finally these measures were codified in legislation in 1597 and 1601, under the terms of which justices could erect houses of correction to deal with beggars and vagrants and the operation of the proposed system of relief was outlined.

Each parish had to appoint two overseers of the poor, who were to work with the churchwardens to care for the poor, set to work those able to do so, and apprentice poor children. Wherever possible family members were to provide financial support. The financial burden for supporting those without family or other means would fall upon their place of residence. Houses of correction would be set up for those refusing to pay poor relief or refusing work. Walthamstow formed part of Becontree Hundred, whose house of correction was at Barking. There remained problems with beggars, and the Act of Settlement of 1662 established the principle of relief by place of settlement. This was gained by birth in the parish, including those born to single mothers, by marrying a husband from the parish, by employment as a servant in the parish for a year, by being apprenticed to an employer resident in the parish or by renting a house worth £10 per year. Anyone needing relief in the parish who did not meet these terms would be subject to an examination by a justice to determine his or her last place of settlement and then despatched there. Parishes were motivated to keep down the costs to ratepayers, and there was a tendency to apprentice orphan children outside the parish boundaries and to move on 'big bellied women' with speed so that their children were born elsewhere. Employment contracts for servants were sometimes limited to prevent them becoming a problem after they were discharged. Litigation between parishes could also result when claims were disputed.

Walthamstow paid for spinning wheels in 1711 to try to recover something from its twenty paupers. From 1699 the parish kept a list of all local poor residents who had legal settlements elsewhere – as a precautionary measure – and the duties of the beadle employed from 1739 included the investigation of anyone coming to live in the parish without a certificate of settlement. Sometimes it was more cost effective to make a single payment – as in 1724 when the churchwarden paid 2s 6d to Mary Swift 'to clear ye parish of her Great Belly'. The parish officers also pursued absent fathers when they could – in 1742 Robert Warton got two months hard labour in the house of correction at Barking for fathering a child on Frances Goodwin, in service in Walthamstow, and also had to pay the parish £6 towards parochial costs.

A PARISH WORKHOUSE

But if the rates were to be kept down then alternatives to payments of poor relief had to be found. In 1711 churchwarden John Bocock submitted costs of £1 6s 6d relating to two separate investigations of finding out 'a way to imploy the poor'. What prompted a solution was legislation of 1723. *An Act for amending the Laws relating to the Settlement, Imployment, and Relief of the Poor*, allowed parishes to rent property for use as a workhouse, and to deny relief to anyone who refused to become an inmate. For those parishes who had already established workhouses, this test resulted in a drop in claims for relief, and in turn lower poor rates. Barking, Romford and Brentwood had already benefited – could not Walthamstow do the same?

The key resolution came on 27 December 1725:

> 'Wheras ye Care & Charge of ye poor begins very sensibly to encrease with in this our parish and wheras the establishing of workhouses in several parts of the nations for entertaining maintaining and Employing therin the poor, hath bene found highly advantagiouse to all respective parishes, as well as Comfortable to the poor themselves. It is therefore resolved and Ordered .... that the present Churchwardens and Overseers of ye poor with Certain other persons... Act as a Committee of Vestry... and treat and agree for a proper House to be taken

for three years from Lady day next, for the reception and Employment of all such poor as shal receive or require legal maintenance of the parish, and that the said house being actually hired and in possession of the parish officers, all such persons as now receive pentions or money for rent, bee forthwith removed and placed by the Overseers of the poor in the said house, those of the alms house only excepted.'

Early in 1726 the committee arranged the lease of a house on Hoe Street from Joseph Schooling. Vestry authorisation was procured to furnish it, Thomas King and his wife employed as the first workhouse master and mistress, and rules were agreed. Immediate expenses were met from the charity of Sigismund Trafford. The workhouse opened in April 1726 and the financial effects were immediate, with settled pensioners on weekly relief dropping from thirty to five, and the costs dropping from £11 6s per month to £2 12s. After three years, the vestry decided to build their own house.

VESTRY HOUSE

Again charity money was drawn on, and stock left to the parish by Thomas Turner and Antony and Dinah Compton, previously used for bread, was sold. The money, augmented by a donation from Thomas Clark, was then used to buy an acre of land on the edge of Church Common, which had come on the market following the bankruptcy of South Sea Company director Sir Jacob Jacobson. The land included the site of the present Spiritualist Church and a path on the line of the present Vestry Road to the north of the railway bridge, and it was probably this path that determined the position of the new building. Builder William Edwards completed a two-storey symmetrical house in a brown stock brick. There were four rooms on the ground floor, with a vestry meeting room on the left and the workhouse master's room at the back, with cooking facilities. On the right were the kitchen and dining area for the inmates. Upstairs were another four rooms, used as dormitories and work space. The build-

78. Vestry House in 1900. Watercolour by A.B. Bamford. The cage is visible on the right of the picture.

79. Entrance to Vestry House showing the inscription over the door.

ing cost £343 12s 3d. An inventory of 1747 shows that there were cellars and a brewhouse, for which a well had been dug in 1742. Over the front door was (and is) a plaque

This house erected
An. Dom MDCCXXX
if any would not work
Neither should he eat

executed by Samuel Chandler, a statuary of Wanstead.

There were four beds and bedsteads with two blankets, a rug to each bed and a small chest in each of the bedrooms. There were 34 inmates, two men, aged 60 and 80, ten women between the ages of 20 and 80, eleven boys and eleven girls. The youngest child was five months old. This population averaged about thirty for the first fifty years of the workhouse, but it was to grow.

A shed was added in 1752, but major alterations followed four years later, when once again the issue of making the poor work had arisen. The vestry borrowed £400, later paid back from rates, which funded a two-storey extension to the west of the original building, providing a long work-room below and a dormitory above. This stood separately from the original building until joined by a covered way in the early nineteenth century. The southern part of the front was extended in 1779 to provide an enlarged vestry room. Work for the inmates meant spinning, laundry and the repair of clothes and possibly shoes, plus labour in the garden and oakum picking. Able-bodied men could sometimes help with building repairs, as they did in 1817 when part of the brickwork of the 'boghole' was taken down and the shaft deepened.

But regimes came and went so that there were regular attempts to find better employment. A committee was set up in 1780, which made recommendations. In 1785 William Dallett, the new master, proposed employing paupers in winding and preparing cotton for tallow chandlers. But in 1831 a visit by the Workhouse Management Committee found only domestic chores being undertaken. Again there were recommendations – yarn to be bought for the children to knit, flannel and linen to be made up by the female inmates as clothing and bedding, and that children should only attend the National school for religious instruction – work should take precedence.

In part this response arose from the rising cost of keeping the poor during the eighteenth century. Numbers gradually rose so that by the 1820s there was an average of eighty inmates. This was in line with the experience of neighbouring parishes in Middlesex. In addition to seeking income from the inmates' labour, the vestry also tried different management systems. After the Kings, workhouse masters and mistresses had other duties – in 1742 John Johnson also acted as beadle, and his wife taught the workhouse children. In 1753 however the then master, Richard Haynes, signed a contract to 'farm the poor', that is to clothe and feed the paupers for a fixed sum per head – in his case 2s 6d per person per week. Of course such contracts were open to competition where the Vestry could accept lower tenders, but the contractor then had the problem of meeting all costs and extracting sufficient income to make it worth while. Haynes' successor Mr Tarlan undercut that rate and also offered to provide bedding, coals, wood, candles and keep brewing vessels in repair, but he soon found he had to go back to the vestry in the face of the rising cost of provisions. Successive contractors faced the same problem, and eventually in 1778 the vestry established a committee to examine the state of the poor.

This committee, under Joel Johnson, a London architect and a member of the Carpenters' Company, drew up new rules for the governance of the house in 1780. The vestry took back direct control of the house, reverting to advertising for a salaried workhouse master and mistress. After one master moved on and another couple were discharged for incompetence, the parish appointed William and Elizabeth Dallett in 1785. William died in harness in 1803, but Elizabeth Dallett was to stay on until 1830. The 1780 reforms included the appointment of separate rooms for sick males and females, and also laid down a new diet. Breakfast was bread and cheese on Sundays, and either milk pottage or broth on other days. Dinner, the midday meal, was puddings and vegetables on Sunday, meat and vegetables on two weekdays, puddings or dumplings on one day, soup on two others and potatoes and cold meat or soup on Saturdays. Supper was bread and cheese or butter.

New clothing was specified in 1776, which was improved in 1780. Men and boys had:

> '2 Coats, 2 Waistcoats one of each to be kept clean for Sunday and the other Coat and Waistcoat for common use all to be made of good Yorkshire Plain of a drab colour with flat Metal Buttons, & 2 Pair of Russia drab Breeches, three shirts, 3 Stocks, three Pair of Stockens, three Coloured Handerkerchiefs, two night Caps, two Pair of shoes, One hat, the Antient Men may have great Coats & the Old women Cloaks if Needfull.'

The female wardrobe included:

> 'A Gown & Quilted Petticoat of Linsee the same colour of the Mens Cloaths, and Extra Gown of the same for Sundays, A Baise Petticoat, A Pair of Leather Bodice, Three shifts, 3 Night Caps, three day caps, 3 Pairs of Stockens, 3 Coloured and one white apron, 3 Coloured & one white Handerkerchief, 2 Pairs of shoes, 2 Pockets, a Straw hat.'

Children were to be taught to read, write , 'cast Accounts' and given the rudiments of religion. The 1780 rules prescribed a start of day for all at half past five in summer and seven o'clock in winter, with bed at nine in summer and eight in winter. Johnson's reforms were to survive until the 1830s, and the workhouse was in general well run. But the cost to the parish continued to rise. In the 1820s inmate numbers were between 48 and 57. The poor rate poundage virtually doubled between 1782 and 1832 and the amount raised virtually quadrupled. Outdoor relief had not been wholly done away with and was a contributory cost – lists of pensioners published monthly may have shamed but it did not prevent people applying. The workhouse regime was seen to have grown too comfortable in the late 1820s, and after a stormy scene with the Committee the widowed Elizabeth Dallett was dismissed in 1830.

It is hard to judge the effect of the new and brief regime that followed, but the Assistant Overseer's day book of 1834-6, the period immediately before the take-over by the new poor law union, records a brick being thrown at the overseer and the illuminating saga of one Joseph Harrington, who had a certificate as to health problems in early July 1834. After a lapse in the procedure, 15 lbs of oakum was delivered to the house in June with the intention of having the inhabitants unpick the strands. Faced with the unpleasant task, Harrington and a companion simply refused to do it. On 11 July they were kept on bread and water and threatened with a committal if they did not give in, but both still refused. On the night of 17 July, Harrington absconded 'takeing with him his bag, scaled the wall about one o'clock this morning'. There was further trouble and abuse from two men who remained, one of whom spent some time in the cage. Then Harrington returned, but the assistant overseer decided that he was better out than in, and refused to admit him. The final entry is on 27 August. 'Joseph Harrington applied for relief. Gave him 2s. He is gone away.'

In the end it was national poor law reform, and a new determination to abolish outdoor relief that overtook all parish workhouses, including Walthamstow's. The old regime had allowed local discretion, and exceptional measures in times of hardship. A bad harvest in 1800 produced exceptional distress, and a shortage of corn, so a general meeting of inhabitants decided to cultivate Markhouse Common field. The owners and occupiers agreed to pay the overseers 10s an acre for bread for the poor as soon as the corn was carried. The poor were also to be supplied with potatoes and cured herrings at a reduced price. In the dogmatic new world of the mid 1830s there would be no place for a homegrown partnership of charity and regulation of the poor.

Laying down the law

A JUSTICE OF THE PEACE

The manor had been the principal unit of administration in medieval Walthamstow, but as we have seen, legislation gradually shifted the balance to the parish. The administration of justice had always been a function wider than the manor, with royal courts for more heinous crimes, and church courts for religious and much of what would now be regarded as civil matters. However the sixteenth century had also seen a growth in the importance of the justice of the peace, appointed from among county men of substance and standing. By the mid seventeenth century, a justice would be expected to attend assizes and quarter sessions, and petty sessions on a monthly basis in his own division of the county. The justice would also have duties to perform in administering the poor law – examination of paupers to ascertain their place of settlement after 1662, validating parish apprenticeships – and a range of other duties, including supervision of the collection of taxation, and at times involvement with the local militia.

William Holcroft was a justice of the peace from 1664 to his death in 1689 and kept a notebook of his activities. Holbrook, born around 1618, lived at Brookscroft, Forest Road for much of his adult life. He had married the widow of a wealthy City merchant, and could spare the time to take part in parish affairs. He served as a Walthamstow churchwarden in 1658, and his gradual acquisition of property made him one of the wealthiest men in the parish at the time of the hearth tax of 1662. A year earlier he had been commissioned a captain in the Essex militia, and became a Waltham Forest verderer in 1668. He joined the bench in 1664, serving alongside men from long established families as well as the more moderate of those who had risen to prominence in the 1650s. He was knighted in 1669. Holcroft kept a note book recording his official business from 1661 to 1688 which provides an insight into law and order in the late seventeenth century.

The militia was seen as a safe alternative to a standing army, and, being raised by the local gentry, was not a drain on national taxation. It would be officered by local gentry, with men drawn on locally, perhaps having four musters per year and serving for no more than a month at a time. But militia duty was unpopular, both with those responsible for finding the money and those forced to serve and in the early 1660s Holcroft was sending out notices to Essex parish constables to distrain the goods of those who had failed to send soldiers. In Holcroft's period the militia saw active service in the Second Dutch War of 1666-7, when it marched to Harwich to defend the port against attack by the Dutch and also defended Tilbury. There was also an active call up in 1685 at the time of Monmouth's rebellion, when Holcroft's company marched from Ilford to Epping and then on to Colchester.

Holcroft's forest business included attendance at a range of courts, whose duties overlapped with manorial courts, on issues like deepening of fords, decay of bridges and neglecting to scour ditches, as well as encroachments for agricultural or building purposes. But there were also criminal matters, including poaching. The collapse of the royal authority in the civil war had led to a near wipe out of deer in the Forest of Waltham, and after the Restoration, poaching remained a severe problem. Holcroft's journal includes many references to the discovery of guns, nets, venison and deerskins in local houses. Nor was all hunting clandestine. In 1684 Jonathan Miller, a Walthamstow resident, was apprehended by the constables for coursing with greyhounds. It is likely that the battle with illicit hunters and poachers was a continuous one.

Crime was not the major problem it was to become in the eighteenth century. There was a bad harvest in 1661 and a rash of property crime, but towards the end of his life crime in the Becontree hundred, which included Walthamstow, gradually rose, probably as a direct result of proximity to London. But this should be put in perspective – there were three grand larcenies, one petty larceny, a burglary, an assault and homicide in the 1660s, plus one prosecution for failing to repair the highway and six more for men setting up as butchers without first serving an apprenticeship.

The most common form of punishment was binding over, and could be used in cases of defamation, assault, or threat of assault. But vagrants, the disorderly or idle local poor, runaway servants, petty thieves or unmarried mothers could be sent to the house of correction at Barking. Offenders could also be sent there pending trial at petty sessions and if found guilty returned there for a spell of hard labour. Holbrook was not the most active of justices, but on one occasion he turned detective. In June 1671 a Mr Terry, living at Winns (now Water House, the William Morris Gallery, but then owned by Dame Mary Pierce), reported that some lead sheets had been stolen from the top of the outer gate. Holcroft had the neighbourhood searched and found '4 greate pieces of leade hiden in a ditch'. He set the local watch on the case, whose vigilance was rewarded when three men came to collect their booty at 10pm. One man claimed the others had told him they had discovered a bargain – the lead lying in a ditch – but Holcroft was not deceived.

Lying hidden on a summer night by a ditch was all part of the duties for the local constables, but they could also be on the wrong end of a stick. In 1673 Thomas Towes, the Walthamstow constable, had received a visit from Thomas Williams, servant to Cheney Rowe at 10pm, offering him 6lbs of candles in exchange for beer, telling Towes that he had managed to obtain these with his master's money in such a way as he thought would remain hidden from Rowe. Towes was sent to confront Williams at Rowes house (Higham Hall), but Williams merely abused him. Rowe' beinge within hearinge came out of his roome wherein he was at dinner and fell voylently upon the complainant [Towes] tellinge him that hee saide hee was a foole, and stroake the complainant severall blowes upon the heade with a cane, and broake the cane upon his heade, Thomas Williams holdinge the complainant's sticke which he had in his hand by the end, soe that he could not get it out of Mr Row's reach.' Rowe later admitted that he had struck the constable and that he had forbidden his servant to bear witness. With gentry involved it is likely that the matter went no further.

EIGHTEENTH-CENTURY CRIME

Much criminal activity in the following century was also fairly minor, such as the case of the vanishing pewter plates from a shelf in the Duke's Head public house in Wood Street in 1765. Sharp-eyed landlord Robert Ashlett did not have to wait long, for while he was pouring a pint for customer John Smith he saw Smith 'take one pewter plate off the shelf and put it into a Pocket in the inside of his coat'. Ashlett's employee Christopher Fish caught Smith and a search revealed two more very dirty plates, which Smith claimed were his and which he hoped to sell to buy clothes. There was trouble of a worse kind at the Cock Tavern

80. The Cock Tavern in 1870. Watercolour by J.T. Wilson

in the late 1760s. In 1767 Joseph Boulter was attacked by some of his drinking companions after he left the tavern and in 1769 a group lay in wait for another customer, William Galpin, after he had taken a pot of beer and beat him up. Later in the same year landlord William Jewerst had shut up the pub for the night when six Irishmen demanded admittance. Jewerst and his companion, Joseph Stratford, a victualler from Whitechapel, refused, whereupon Jewerst was struck and had his collar bone broken. Despite injuries both men locked the door but the would-be drinkers broke the windows and tried to force an entry.

Somehow the local constable was roused, though by the time he arrived at the Cock the rioters had gone. Despite his injuries, Jewerst went with the constable to look for the men, heading to the most likely destination, a lodging house kept by another Irishman, Philip Brauning, possibly in the area of the present Westbury Road. The six were not there, but as a host of lodgers came down in their night shirts to see what the fuss was about, a hail of bricks was thrown from a field opposite. One struck the unfortunate Jewerst on the back of the head and he was carried back to his pub in a bad way. The local surgeon, Charles Briscoe of the Red House, was not summoned until the following morning, and although he did his best, including letting blood, the injury to the skull proved ultimately fatal, for Jewerst died ten months later.

THE JEFFRIES MURDER

Walthamstow's most celebrated eighteenth century crime was the Jeffries murder. In 1742, Joseph Jeffries, a wealthy butcher, had taken in his fifteen-year-old niece, Elizabeth. Whatever his original intentions to her were, Jeffries subjected Elizabeth to sexual abuse. In her early twenties she started an affair with her uncle's man servant, John Swan, three years her senior. Her uncle got wind of it and threatened to cut his niece out of his will. Fearing destitution Elizabeth persuaded Swan to murder Jeffries. An initial attempt with arsenic failed, and a vagrant they had hoped to pay to carry out the deed refused, so the pair had to take drastic action. One night in July 1751 the pair faked a robbery, taking some brass items and throwing them in a nearby pond. Swan shot his master in the head and Elizabeth raised the alarm pretending that robbers had carried out the attack.

Initially all was well, but then the sack of

81. John Swan and Elizabeth Jeffryes.

supposed loot was found. Neighbours said that a whole hour had gone by between the shot being fired and Elizabeth's cries of alarm (she had fallen asleep waiting for her accomplice to return). Elizabeth had been very eager to take possession of a deed box after her uncle's death. Finally the vagrant, Thomas Matthews, came forward as a witness. Elizabeth and her lover were arrested and tried at Chelmsford on 11 March 1752. Both were found guilty and sentenced to hang. They were drawn back in a hurdle on a slow journey from Chelmsford to a gibbet near Leyton High Stone, where a huge crowd had gathered. Elizabeth's body was claimed by her friends and buried, but Swan's was left to hang in chains until the local gentry complained, after which it was removed to the Bald Face Stag at Buckhurst Hill. The whole story was turned into a BBC radio drama in the dark days of the Second World War.

CAGING AND WATCHING

Perhaps it was the drink related crime in Marsh Street, but in 1765 the vestry resolved to provide some temporary accommodation for those apprehended by the constables prior to their appearance before a magistrate. Accordingly a small watch house – 'The Cage', was built against the east wall of Vestry House. This measured eight feet square with a sloping roof rising to six foot at the eaves. There was a small barred window on the east wall and a door on the south side. It was not intended for lengthy detentions, although offending workhouse inmates occasionally spent short periods there. Special precautions were taken when dangerous criminals were housed there as in 1792 when four men guarded Henry Cornhill, a footpad. The Cage survived to be used by the Metropolitan Police, but in the later nineteenth century it was put to a variety of uses, including stabling a horse, before it was demolished in 1912. Today cement lines show the line of the pitch roof on the Museum.

In 1819 concern over rising crime led the parish to set up a Patrol and Watch Committee. Supported by local subscription, the Committee established armed night patrols, including one or two horsemen and eight men on foot to operate at night in the winter. Case records survive. Some time before 1am on the morning of Sunday 21 October 1821, the Superintendent, Francis Penn and two members of the patrol encountered one William Brewer near the present High Street junction with Pretoria Avenue. Brewer

> insulted him as Constable and Patrol, by using most abusive language upon which Penn seized him by the collar, and with the assistance of Patmore brought him to the Cage and locked him up, from which he made his escape on Sunday Afternoon between 3 & 4 o'Clock by sawing through the lining of the Cage and forcing out the Brick Work of the wall nine inch in thickness.

Patmore also gave evidence to support Penn, claiming that Brewer had been:

> 'Snapping his fingers and saying he would as lief kill him (meaning as they suppos'd, Penn) as eat hisVictuals; that he was the fattest of the three and ought to be killed first.'

Five days later, at about the same early hour, Penn heard a disturbance in the street and found his patrol threatened by two Excisemen. He warned them off, but on his way home he was fired at by Brewer's brother James, who was with armed companions. Somehow Penn escaped and James Brewer was later arrested at his house two days later on the Saturday, and his brother was recaptured in a Clapton alehouse on Sunday. This time no chances were taken and William was despatched post haste to Barking gaol.

PARISH AND METROPOLITAN POLICE

During the disturbed period of 1830-31 that preceded the limited reform of the franchise of 1832, the patrols were also on day duty. When the vestry adopted the Watching and Lighting Act of 1830, the patrol system was replaced by a sergeant and a squad of constables, paid for from the watching and lighting rate. This ceased in 1833, and the subscription system, in the form of a voluntary rate and the old committee was revived for two years. In 1835 the parish adopted the Lighting and Watching Act of 1833, but applied it only to that part of the parish south of Clay Street and Haggar Lane - presuming that the more rural area to the north was less likely to be disturbed. This force survived until 1840, when Walthamstow was included in the Metropolitan Police area.

The best of the parish constables were taken into the new N Division, and the police leased the northern part of Vestry House from the parish. A new internal cell was built, and the station complement consisted of four sergeants, seventeen foot patrols and one horse patrol constable. Seven cottages were built shortly after 1840. The four at the bottom of the present Museum garden were demolished in 1967, but one pair, and the sergeant's house survived to be converted into museum offices in 1979-80. The police connection ended when a new police station on Lea Bridge Road was completed in 1869 and all staff transferred the following year.

Every area has had its share of sensational crime and late Victorian Walthamstow was no exception. In 1883 William Gouldstone, a whitesmith working in Upper Thames Street, but living with his family in Courtenay Place, St James Street murdered his six children, shortly after his wife had given birth to twins. Gouldstone was convicted of murder and sentenced to death, but was diagnosed as insane and reprieved, being confined to an asylum. In 1895 Florence Rolph, aged six, was sent from her home in Browns Road to bring back a full can of beer for her father. The journey to the nearest public house, the Rose and Crown, was a mere eighty yards, but she did not return, and a search later found her body in the grounds of Rectory Manor, then unoccupied. The child had been raped and suffocated. The route between the pub and the grounds led past at least eighty small houses, so it was assumed at the time that Florence knew her attacker, since no-one remembered a man dragging an unwilling child. But there were no witnesses and no one was ever convicted for the murder.

82. *Rear of police cottages behind Vestry House, 1977.*

A criminal event that truly made the headlines was the 'Tottenham Outrage'. On 23 January 1909 a pair of anarchists robbed a vehicle carrying wages to a Tottenham factory. The gang were chased across the Lea and along Forest Road. They boarded a tram standing at Highams Station Avenue passing loop, which was ready for the return journey to the Baker's Arms. The driver escaped upstairs but a passenger was shot in the neck and the anarchists forced the conductor to drive at gun point. Police commandeered a second tram and followed in hot pursuit. Abandoning the tram the duo took to a passing milk cart, heading towards Hale End. One was shot by police and the other burst into a cottage next to the Royal Oak and took a child into an upstairs room as hostage. The stand off ended when the man committed suicide. Strangely the stolen money was never recovered – there was nothing on either of the bodies, and yet they had had no time to hide it.

On a more cheerful note, in the following year the police picked up the tab for an unexpected delivery. On 10 February 1910 a local woman gave birth on a tram in Markhouse Road, and the conductor, a Walthamstow Urban District Council employee, summoned a doctor. Naturally in the pre National Health Service era, the doctor looked to receive payment for his services, and as they had been requested by a Council employee, he sent the bill to the Council. However it was the Council's view that maternity services on moveable council property should not be met from the rates, and that the matter should be viewed as one for the forces of law and order. Surprisingly the police paid up! Perhaps it was simply the course of least resistance.

Travelling and Travellers

ROADS INTO TURNPIKES

Before the early eighteenth century, maintaining roads was a parish responsibility, whether the road was a minor lane, or a highway of national importance. Under the powers of an Act of Parliament of 1555, parishes could oblige local residents to take part in organised maintenance (statutory labour), although the better off paid for substitutes. The work was supervised by an elected official, the surveyor of the highways. The results were very variable and journeys could be lengthy, impeded by quagmires in winter and dust and pot holes in summer. No main roads (king's highways) crossed Walthamstow, but road traffic gradually increased as the eighteenth century progressed and the better-off who had houses in Walthamstow wanted better communications than the ferries across the Lea could provide.

A model for how roads could be improved already existed in the turnpike trusts. Roads were administered by trusts, which had the powers to erect gates and charge road users a toll that could go towards repairs. Initially seen as a temporary measure, early trusts had their terms extended by later legislation. The model that others followed was set up in 1706. The Great Essex Road from Chelmsford and Romford, which crossed the Lea at Bow Bridge, became the responsibility of the Middlesex and Essex Trust in 1724, together with what is now the A11, through Woodford, and also the road from Stratford through Leytonstone to the High Stone. Walthamstow's own trust focused on the problem of crossing the Lea, but naturally road improvement was also required.

By the early eighteenth century there was a ferry and a bridge to Tottenham at the Ferry Boat inn, and a smaller ferry across the Lea from Higham Hill. Just south of the Walthamstow border, Butterfields Lane, on roughly the same alignment as the present Lea Bridge Road, had once taken travellers to the Lockbridge and ford to cross to Clapton. But the bridge was not kept in a proper state of repair and had collapsed by

83. In early times a ferry took travellers from London across the Lea to Walthamstow. This is a view of Walthamstow from the river in 1934, by T. Stuart Milner.

84. The second Lea Bridge, as pictured in 1821.

1630. A wooden causeway that crossed the drainage channels in the marshes had connected with the bridge. Repaired by George Monoux in the early sixteenth century, this was in ruins by the 1580s. The Lockbridge was replaced by the Lockbridge ferry, later known as Jeremy's Ferry. In 1757 local people obtained an Act of Parliament to replace the ferry with a bridge and to improve roads at Snaresbrook and Clapton, among them Butterfields Lane.

LEA BRIDGE AND ROAD TURNPIKE TRUST

The old road was replaced by a new one, forty foot wide, with toll gates and houses. Jeremy's ford was destroyed. A toll house was put up on the Hackney side of the new wooden bridge and the tolls were auctioned to private contractors periodically. Later alterations including straightening the Chestnut Walk part of the road, that section between Shernhall Street and Whipps Cross in 1814. By 1819 the original wooden bridge was showing signs of wear, with some of the wooden piers threatening to collapse. This posed a dilemma for the trustees, since a new iron bridge would cost £3,600 and would require a new Act of Parliament. This Act was duly obtained, but gave the trustees only a 21-year period and imposed new duties on the trustees of watching and lighting the road and bridge. Work on the second bridge began in 1820 and it opened on 25 March 1821, with a new set of tolls to help meet the costs.

STAGE COACHES

The new road allowed considerable improvements to Walthamstow's route to London, as the promoters had hoped. John Gibson of Walthamstow had run a stage coach service linking Walthamstow and Leyton in 1707. This business was probably taken over by Joseph Schooling snr prior to 1731 and provided a route to the City of London via Stratford. Schooling was still running on this route in 1758, when he advertised the business for sale. The Schooling house and coach yard were on the site of 192-202 High Street, and the sale included 'Glass Coaches and Chariots, a black Coach and a Hearse and Horses and all good Utensils belonging to the Stage Coach Yards.'

The purchaser was Francis Wragg senior, who took advantage of the new turnpike to re-route the coaches. Wragg (1713-82) was the first of four family members to run the business, the others being his nephew Francis (1747-95), Francis's nephew Robert (1776-1861) and Robert's son Francis (1806-91), and their business was to last until 1880. Robert was also a corndealer and farmer, occupying the Clay Street farm on the site of the present Waltham Forest civic offices. By the 1820s Robert also let out post horses, chaises and flys, and supplied horses for road repair to the Lea Bridge and Road Trust. By 1850 Robert had moved to the Nags Head in Walthamstow village, and was also described as an omnibus proprietor

There are few details of the early level of services, though by 1825 there were nine daily return journeys to the City. In 1826 coaches left from the Nag's Head and the Chequers in the High Street at 8am, 9am, 10am and returned at 3pm, 5pm, 6pm and 8pm in the evening from the Green Dragon in Bishopsgate. The hours had varied by 1834, but there were then five return journeys on Sundays. Coaches could not pick up or set down at intermediate stops in that area of central London within the Bills of Mortality and costs were high, with new coaches costing £100, horses £20 each (and expected to last no more than four years) and with 15 shillings per week spent on feed for each horse. Accommodation was limited. In 1836 Wragg's coach to the Royal Exchange housed six people inside and twelve outside, while the coach to Bishopsgate had reduced external space for only nine people. These top seats were exposed to all weathers – not pleasant on a wet and windy day when crossing the marshes. In 1839 a coach owned by J. Pitt also ran from Chingford to the Royal Exchange.

The Lea Bridge Trust was one of those amalgamated into the Metropolis Roads Commission in 1827, who found their new acquisition to be well maintained compared to other London trust roads. The Commission also undertook work on a new road from Whipps Cross. This road, the Woodford New Road, linking Snaresbrook Road to Woodford Green, opened in 1830. Not all of the Commission's proposals came to fruition – they also wished to build a major new road connecting Seven Sisters Road (completed in 1831) to the Epping New Road at Fairmead Bottom. This highway would have gone from Tottenham across the Lea at the Ferry Boat inn, over Higham Hill Common to the present Larkshall Road and then via Chingford Hatch alongside the course of the Ching. Had it been built it would have altered the development of Walthamstow, possibly moving the focus of later building further north, but the Commission did not get permission to proceed. In part this may have been due to the early impact of the new railway developments, among which was the Northern & Eastern Railway Bill, which went before Parliament in 1836.

THE FIRST LOCAL RAILWAYS

It was this bill that was to give Walthamstow its first rail connection. The new line ran along the Lea Valley linking Broxbourne to Bishopsgate, with a local station at Lea Bridge and a new bridge to carry the turnpike road over the railway, carefully concealing the engines and carriages from passing horse traffic by a high wall. The station building was on the new bridge, with steps leading down to the platforms until 1949 when it was destroyed in a fire. The sponsoring company leased its line to the Eastern Counties Railway in 1844, itself to become one of the constituents of the Great Eastern Railway in 1862.

The new line left much of Walthamstow a considerable distance from a station, and in 1844 a rival company, the London & Blackwall, promoted a line to Epping. The Eastern Counties counter-attacked with a proposal of their own, much of which would have followed the present Chingford line, but once they had seen off the competition, the scheme was allowed to drop.

The opening of the new station at Lea Bridge had an immediate effect on Wragg's stage coach service, which ceased its direct run to the City. However the standard of train service did not meet the expectations of some residents and in 1849 there was a move to bring back the City coaches, with twenty people eventually agreeing to subscribe to the service. One service started from Wood Street, the others probably linked High Street and Church End as before. The experiment would appear to have been short lived and probably ceased soon after 1851. Eastern Counties trains were regarded by contemporaries as slow, dangerous and uncomfortable – a cartoon of the 1850s showed a donkey taking on the Eastern Counties train – and winning. The level of the train service was intended to cater for those with businesses in the City. In 1842 there were no morning trains leaving for Bishopsgate before 9am and only one between 8 and 9am in 1861.

With no railway line any closer to Walthamstow, the Wragg business continued to run coaches to Lea Bridge Station. Gilbert Houghton, born in 1852, and whose father was a solicitor practising in Bishopsgate and Walthamstow, recalled childhood memories of his father 'standing by the side of the road in his great-coat, and with his travelling rug over his arm' waiting for the London coach. The children would sometimes watch out for it as it rattled down Wood Street so that William Houghton could sally out and hail it at the Wyatt's Lane corner.

RAILWAY SCHEMES

Some local interests continued to press for a better line. Some wanted a direct link with the City, others saw that inducing people to leave over crowded inner London areas for Walthamstow would increase the value of land in any ensuing phase of building. One set of promoters persuaded Edward Warner, who had become lord of the manor of Higham Bensted in 1849 and was set to become one of the largest local landowners, to support their scheme, the Woodford Railway. In competition with another Eastern Counties scheme, this line would have linked Woodford via Leyton to the City, but would have served the north-eastern part of Walthamstow. Had it been successful, it would have changed the history of the later development in the area, with building starting near Woodford, so perhaps Hale End and not Hoe and High streets would have become the main shopping areas. Epping Forest would have been threatened with building and much more might have gone. But Parliament voted for the alternative route (now part of the Central Line) with stations at Snaresbrook and Loughton. The new line may have benefited the better off inhabitants of Whipps Cross, who could now use Snaresbrook station, but was less useful to Chingford and central Walthamstow residents.

James Higham, a local developer, was among those who put forward yet another scheme, the Walthamstow, Clapton and City Railway in 1864. While Higham was later to oppose workmen's trains, he had hoped for a line which would provide some better class tenants for his houses, which the subsidised horse-bus service had failed to do. However it was to be the workmen who were to provide the incentive to the successful scheme. The Great Eastern Railway, which surfaced from the mergers of 1862, projected the creation of a network of suburban lines and an improved terminus at Liverpool Street. Two lines were proposed, one from Leyton to High Beech, the other from Hackney Downs, joining the first near Wood Street. Despite the lack of lines, parts of south and central Walthamstow had seen well-to-do suburban development and had the potential for far greater building – and levels of traffic. So the second line was projected as a high density one with the strong likelihood of workmen's fares, while the first, intended for business travellers and excursionists to Epping Forest, would have had lesser levels of traffic.

THE CHINGFORD BRANCH

It was the GER schemes that won through in 1864. The company was obliged to tunnel under the National School's playground at Church End, but Walthamstow Common was not saved. It had already seen some recent building, as a small diagonal road cut across it with four houses. Now it was to be bisected by an open cutting, with the houses demolished and the road diverted. This provoked considerable local opposition, but the resulting compromise did not save the common. Alternative space was provided for a recreation ground in Selborne Road, and the residue of the common left over by the railway became a children's playground. Covered by tarmac and with a high mesh fence, it serves this function over 130 years later.

Although the capital was raised, work proceeded slowly on the Walthamstow line until 1867, when funds ran out and the contractors' skips were abandoned on the earthworks near St James Street. Parliamentary pressure brought about a revision of the original schemes. All the High Beech line was abandoned except for the section between Wood Street and Chingford Green, where a new terminus was projected in an Act of 1869. The GER upgraded a spur at Lea Bridge to provide a link to the course to St James Street and on 26 April 1870 commenced a service on the first part of the line to be finished, with stations at St James Street, Hoe Street and ending at a temporary terminus in a cutting west of Shernhall Street. The company acquired a house on the north side of Summit Road, which became the temporary station, giving passengers access down steps into the cutting to the platforms.

In 1872 the link via Hackney Downs was completed at Copper Mill junction and in February 1873 trains terminated at the newly completed Liverpool Street station. There were also changes to the branch route to the east, as local landowner Sir James Vallentin had compelled the company to buy his house, Shern Lodge, and all its grounds (which extended along the whole length of the present Vallentin Road). In turn this allowed the GER to avoid a multiplicity of purchases of small property near the Duke's Head at Wood Street. Now only the sharp wing northwards to reach Wood Street station gives any indication that the branch was planned as anything other than one railway. The temporary terminus went out of use in November 1873 when the line opened to Bull Lane, Chingford with intervening stations at Wood Street and Hale End (renamed Highams

85. Hoe Street Station c.1870. Tinted ink drawing.

86. Thornton Lodge on the north side of Summit Road was taken over by the railway company as a temporary station. Watercolour 1862.

87. Highams Park station. Watercolour by D.E. Phillips, 1937.

Park in 1894, Highams Park and Hale End from 1894-1969 and Highams Park thereafter)

One effect of the new line was the termination of Wragg's coach to Lea Bridge station, which ceased with the opening of Hoe Street station in 1870, though Wragg continued to hire out flys and chaises until his final retirement in 1880.

The dream of reaching High Beech was finally abandoned in 1883. If the 1864 scheme had been implemented it is likely that Highams Park in its present form and name, with no station would not have existed. A station at the Shernhall Street/ Church Lane junction could have shifted local shops away from Wood Street and would have accelerated development round the area of the present Walthamstow village. Now it was to be the Chingford branch which was to have a critical impact on the development of Walthamstow as a whole, as we shall see in the next chapter. The key to this development was the fare structure. The GER imposed higher third class and season ticket prices on the line as a whole, but cheaper workmen's fares – but these extended only as far as Wood Street. The impact of the new line and its fare structure can be seen by comparing the daily passenger statistics. In 1861 only 475 people in winter and 420 in summer travelled from Lea Bridge at a time when Walthamstow's population was over 7,000. By 1902 there were 21,802 daily London travellers out of a population of 100,000.

THE TOTTENHAM & FOREST GATE RAILWAY

Edward Warner's Woodford railway had failed. But his son, Sir Thomas Courtenay Theydon Warner had better fortune, when he acted as the main local promoter for the Tottenham & Forest Gate Railway, sanctioned in 1890. The stated aims were to provide a direct link to King's Cross and encourage Somers Town residents to move out to Walthamstow, using the line to commute into work. The real incentive was goods traffic between the Midland Railway network and the London docks. The *Walthamstow Guardian* thought that what was really needed was a direct link to Victoria station and said so in an editorial in April 1890, but the Midland Railway had its way, and the new six-mile line from Tottenham to Woodgrange Park, with stations at Blackhorse Road, Queens Road, Midland Road, Leyton and Leytonstone, opened in July 1894. This was to be the last of Walthamstow's new railways for over sixty years – there were a number of attempts to revive a line to Epping in the 1880s and 1890s and a tube scheme in the late 1890s for north-east London. But in each case Parliamentary approval could not be obtained.

THE END OF THE TURNPIKES

One of the factors in the fate of these lines was lack of funds, but there had also been changes in roads and road transport. The Metropolis Roads Commission was abolished in 1872 and the roads under its control had dropped down to 67 miles from the original 131 miles. The Lea Bridge Road saw a heavy growth in manure traffic in the 1860s, as the by-product of London's cab trade and carriages went to fertilise Essex farms. This imposed more wear on the road, and accordingly it was repaired with granite chippings. In 1872 responsibility for the road passed to the Hackney, Leyton and Walthamstow parishes and the turnpike tolls were finally abolished. The surviving records of the old trust passed to Walthamstow and were added to the parish records. Standards of road maintenance in general were not high on the list of priorities of Walthamstow's local board, since traffic could now use the new railway from Hoe Street. Lea Bridge Road, along with other major ones in the area, became a county responsibility in 1888 and the Middlesex and Essex County Councils met the bulk of the cost of rebuilding the second Lea Bridge with the present one in 1897.

TRAMS

A horse tram service promoted by the North Metropolitan Tramways Company reached Stratford in 1869. Leytonstone was connected in 1871. The Epping Forest Act of 1878 signalled the opening of the Forest to the public and in 1879 a syndicate was formed to build a tramway to take advantage of the anticipated growth in traffic. Part of the proposal of the Lea Bridge, Leyton & Walthamstow Tramways Company included a horse-powered route along the Lea Bridge Road from a junction with the North Metropolitan's lines at Clapton to the Rising Sun public house on Woodford New Road. Obstacles over the narrow end of Lea Bridge Road at Clapton raised by Hackney's Local Board of Works, were overcome and the Lea Bridge line as far as Whipps Cross was completed on 7 May 1883, with a service beginning five days later. Income was not sufficient to complete the extension to the Rising Sun. The contractors, themselves bankrupted, made successive petitions to be paid or have the company wound up. Services had ceased by October 1884 and for the next five years the track deteriorated with the ten red and white single decked cars lying idle in Clapton terminus.

The project was revived through the efforts of William Griffiths, a Kingsland Road stone merchant. Leyton Local Board had wanted to take over the line, but in the end Griffiths and some colleagues formed a successor company, incorporating the assets of its predecessors in 1888. The existing line was revived, with a new service starting in October 1888. The line to the Rising Sun opened in May 1889, with stables near the Baker's Arms. The Hoe Street line was not built, but a horse-bus service was started. Twelve new double decker trams were bought and by 1899 the company had 75 buses and trams. A legal challenge to the right of tram operators to run bus services in the 1890s prompted the company to hive off its profitable bus operations to a separate company, and this affected profitability, since the trams had to some extent been subsidised by bus income. By the turn of the century both Leyton and Walthamstow urban district councils were interested in setting up electric tram services themselves, though both had difficulties to overcome running services outside their own areas. In the end Leyton purchased the company's lines, except for that on the Hackney part of the Lea Bridge Road, which was scheduled to be acquired by the London County Council. Leyton pushed ahead with electrification, and completed its programme on 1 December 1906. In 1909 Leyton opened a new electrified route

88. A horse tram outside the Rising Sun c.1900, ready to make the return trip to Hackney.

89. A horse tram struggles through floods on the Lea Bridge Road in June 1903 after a sixty-hour storm, which began on Saturday 13 June. It was not until the following Tuesday that this Leyton tram could get through to Hackney.

from Chingford to Stratford, shared with Walthamstow.

Walthamstow UDC had obtained its own Light Railways Order in 1903 for services from the Ferry Boat inn along Forest Road to the Napier Arms, Woodford, from the Baker's Arms via Hoe Street to Chingford Mount, from Markhouse Road via St James Street, Blackhorse Road to Higham Hill and from Waterworks Corner, Woodford to the Rising Sun, a total of about eight miles. The system, including a new depot on Chingford Road, was opened on 3 June 1905, with a five-minute service on the first three routes. There were some problems in getting the overhead cables under the railway bridge at St James Street, and the sharp dip the road still takes under that bridge is the result of the lowering of the road in 1904. The 32 tram cars were double-deckers, with an open top and painted in dark brown and cream, with red shaded numerals. By the early 1920s they were in a poor state of repair after minimal maintenance and hard work during the First World War. One local tram enthusiast compared the service to 'a seedy down at heel character who made good'. After 1922 they were rebuilt and gradually the top decks were covered in between 1928 and 1932. Six new double-deckers were ordered in 1910 for the Chingford to Stratford service, eight single-deck cars – the only ones of their type in East London – were acquired from Rotherham in 1919 to deal with post-war problems, and a further six secondhand London United open top vehicles came in the following year. The fleet was much improved by twenty cars ordered in 1926 and 1932.

The Walthamstow and Leyton services passed to the newly formed London Passenger Transport Board in 1933. Trolleybuses replaced trams between 1936 and 1937, and Walthamstow depot saw the scrapping of many East London trams in the succeeding year. It subsequently became the main bus garage until changes in the structure of bus operations made it redundant in the 1980s. Omnibus Way now occupies the site of the tram and bus sheds, while the office building has been converted into flats.

RAIL SERVICES

Railways remained the main route to London, but conditions on the trains gradually worsened in the years before the First World War. Many workmen did not have to be in to work before 8.30am, but caught the early train with workmen's fares to save money, spending their free time having sandwich breakfasts and smoking on Liverpool Street station. For those going in on later trains, there were only eight out of fifteen carriages with third class stock, and these were highly over-crowded, so that second-class travellers complained of invasions of their carriages by third-class passengers unable to find any space in the third class. The situation had been made worse rather than better by the electric trams, which encouraged the development of northern Walthamstow, and fed into stations south of Wood Street. Passengers squeezed into the guard's compartment, where they paid a °d supplement to the guard for the dubious privilege and boys were known to be loaded up on to luggage racks inside the carriages.

Traffic continued to grow after the First World War. The bulk of second-class passengers before 1914 had been clerks, shop keepers, managers and civil servants, with artisans, warehousemen, postmen and a host of labourers travelling third. In the 1920s they were joined by an increasing number of women, working as typists, clerks or telephonists in central London, and in Hackney and Bethnal Green in shops, the clothing trade or industry. The decade also saw a rise in price of the loss making workmen's fares, though they were not abolished until 1960. Second-class fares went in 1937 and first-class in 1941.

The GER did make efforts to improve services. Track, signalling and siding capacity improvements enabled the introduction of the 'Jazz Services' from 1 January 1920. This entailed 38 sets of coaches, 18 locomotives and 29 extra men for the Enfield and Chingford line services providing 24 peak hour trains, a substantial improvement on the wartime timetable. To ensure rapid loading and turn around times, carriages were colour coded above the doors and coaling and watering facilities improved at the country terminuses. The earlier GE 2-4-2 tanks were supplemented and finally supplanted by the new London & North Eastern Railway N7 0-6-2 tanks which had first appeared as an experimental design by the GER's mechanical engineer A.J. Hill in 1915. The class had a greater reserve of power for the heavier trains, and were economical on water and coal. By 1928 there were 112 of them and they ran the services until electrification in 1960.

The train also provided travel for pleasure as well as work. Excursion traffic became commonplace in the 1930s and by the 1950s there were Sunday summer services to Southend and normally one other service to seaside resorts like Clacton, Brighton or Worthing. There were also football specials on Saturdays and even a connection to Lea Bridge for the Speedway in the 1950s.

The Jazz Services improved conditions, but in the end it was the growth of local employment opportunities in the 1920s and 1930s in local factories that began to diminish the number of commuters. Walthamstow's population also began to decline from its peak of 132,972 in 1931.

NATIONALISATION AND ELECTRIFICATION

Nationalisation of the railways in 1948 saw a revival of the recommendations of the 1926 Traffic Advisory Committee on electrification of the Chingford line. But the high cost delayed the work until the late 1950s. Electrification was finally complete in 1960, and in the same year diesel multiple units replaced steam on the Tottenham & Forest Gate line. This line had lost its Moorgate connection before 1931 and seen a slow decline in the frequency of services. From 1981 its western terminal became Gospel Oak. The aspirations of an earlier age for a direct link to Victoria also resurfaced when Parliament approved the creation of the Victoria underground line in 1955. This was originally intended to start at Wood Street, with a new station at the junction of High Street and Hoe Street, but in the event it started at the existing Hoe Street station, with a rail connection to the Tottenham & Forest Gate line at Blackhorse Road. The new tube line opened in two stages in 1968.

After electrification British Rail gradually rebuilt some of the stations. Wood Street and St James Street were replaced in 1972-3 and Highams Park in 1979. As part of the works for the completion of the Victoria Line the main entrance at Hoe Street was altered, with the new booking office on the Selborne Road side becoming the main ticket office. Selborne Road was partially closed to provide a terminus for a new bus station, which was altered again when the new Selborne Walk shopping centre opened in 1988.

Victorian vigour: developing a suburb

GROWTH AND POPULATION

"It will not be long before the whole of the land between Edmonton and Woodford and Wanstead down to Stratford and Poplar marks a new phase in the development of English local life with a unity more like a county than a borough".

W.S. Clarke's prediction in his *Suburban homes of London* of 1881 was realised in twenty years and Walthamstow became a suburb of London, though in the process also attracting industry and reducing the high proportion of its population dependent on commuting to the City and central London.

The building of the Chingford branch, combined with workmen's fares removed the final obstacle to the development of Walthamstow. Population figures show the rate of growth:

1801: 3006	1851: 4989
1811: 3777	1861: 7137
1821: 4304	1871: 11,092
1831: 4258	1881: 22,531
1841: 4873	1891: 47,454

DEVELOPMENTS OF THE 1850s

The station at Lea Bridge did not make much material difference to the development of the parish, although it made it possible for men like William Houghton to reach his offices in the City and return home at night. However the enclosure of Markhouse Common, Higham Hill Common and the Church Common in 1850 led to the creation of new roads later used by developers. In the south of Boundary Road and Queens Road were built to join Markhouse Road and Hoe Street. At Higham Hill, Blackhorse Lane and the former Common Lane, elevated to High Hill Road, became public roads, and a new road, St Andrew's Road, was built between them. Common Lane, leading from Hoe Street to Church Street, became Orford Road, and the footpath crossing the common was diverted to run diagonally.

Grazing rights on the commons were abolished, but there was neither the funding nor the tenants for wholesale development at this stage. At Church Common, the north-west part was reserved for a recreation ground, while a part to the south of Orford Road was used for gravel digging. Some larger houses were built round the common - Comely Bank to the east of the present Beulah Path, and Avenue House, on the site of the present row of shops on the south side of Orford Road, east of Wingfield Road (and replaced by those shops in 1890). Summit Road was laid out on the former Sandpit Field and the first

90. Palissy House on Markhouse Road, watercolour by J.C. Barralet (1814-90). It was built in 1880-1 for William Barralet (1826-1914) who had retired at the age of 50 from a sanitary ware business and who moved from Sidney Cottage next to the Common Gate public house once Palissy House was completed. His new house stood next to another family enterprise, the builders' merchant business next to 41 Markhouse Road. Barralet served on Walthamstow's local board and owned the Walthamstow Herald. A socialist, he was visited here by George Bernard Shaw.

cottage built and occupied by 1851. Marion Villas, paired semi-detached houses, were built opposite each other on the diverted footpath – they were to be short lived, being demolished when the railway was cut through in 1869.

Other development of the 1850s and 1860s included Union and Prospect Roads on Markhouse Common in 1852, the felling of the elm avenue that led to Grosvenor House for the construction of Grosvenor Park Road in 1851, and the loss of another avenue of trees to build the present East and West Avenues. Near the Church Common, Beulah, Eden and Pembroke Roads were laid out. Orford Road had once been a cart track to the common, but in 1853-6 several large houses were built on it, including Comely Bank, now used as a health centre, which stands on the east side of Beulah Path. Roads on the Tower Hamlets estate were laid out from 1851, with the bulk of the houses constructed from 1855 to 1859.

Elsewhere development had begun under the auspices of speculative land societies, who laid out streets and plots, which small builders acquired, and which were bought and tenanted by newcomers, mostly from London. Some of the funding came from building societies. The earliest were the Walthamstow First and Second Building Societies, founded about 1844, which like many such societies operating over the next thirty years were terminating ones. Members paid in small weekly sums, which were allocated by ballot and the society ended once the last member had received an allocation of funds. The amounts loaned were likely to be small, being in the £150 to £300 range, as were the totals – the WF & SB Societies had advanced £5,400 and £3,800 by 1861. Permanent building societies became more popular, and there were other bodies, like the Land, Building, Investment and Cottage Improvement Society, whose directors included two developers, Ebenezer Clarke jnr and Benjamin Rowbotham, but terminating societies were still being formed in the 1880s.

FINANCE

Partly this was due to the emphasis placed on security by the permanent societies, which then had difficulties finding suitable property to lend against. There were exceptions, like the Temperance Permanent Building Society, which by 1861 had advanced £4000 against cottage property – but this may have had more to do with Ebenezer Clarke, who was also a director. The 1880s saw the opening of bank branches in the area – but bank loans were a risky source of capital for the speculative builder in that loans could be rapidly called in, and lead to bankruptcy. More capital came from the savings of local businessmen, including publicans. Landowners would lay out roads, but could also advance money to local builders, while companies could loan the purchases price of plots, to place less of a financial burden on the builders.

All of this was also set against national financial cycles, with peaks in the late 1860s, 1878-80 and 1900, and slumps in 1873 and 1891. Builders could expect rocky rides – G. Willsmer was insolvent in 1860, bankrupt in 1863 and 1871 and in the late 1870s he lost an action against Leyton Local Board over infringement of the building regulations and liquidated his firm. He was running a timber business from Hoe Street station yard in 1883, but was back building property in the area in the following decade.

LAND AND LANDLORDS

The lack of good rail links slowed the development of the northern part of the parish, but physical and environmental factors could also affect estate growth. Walthamstow's Local Board succeeded in defeating the proposals put forward in 1888-91 to use a large area of the undeveloped north for a cemetery, and John Hitchman was then able to develop the St John's and Wadham estates in the ensuing decades. Problems with poor drainage could slow development – for example on the Clay Street farm land, where the Town Hall basements (built on the site) used to flood in the 1960s, and the Coppermill estate. This was built on low-lying land which William Houghton had thought of no value for building purposes at an enquiry of 1897. Six roads were proposed for the site but by 1897 only three had been laid out. 45 houses had been built by that year, but in comparison to other estates, progress was slow and remained so five years later. Similarly the ease of extraction of brick earth locally helped, but was not a major factor.

Finally there were the attitudes and aspirations of the landlords. At one end were owners like Samuel Bosanquet, who missed out on the opportunities for development altogether, and apart from some small sales to the British Land Company and the disposal of Low Hall farm to the local board, still leased the remainder of his estate for farming in 1889. Others like Sir Robert Fitzwygram took an active role and used the building lease to exercise a degree of control over what was built. Some estates remained in limbo while legal disputes were settled, as with the Belle Vue estate and the Walthamstow Park estate, whose co-owners had to agree the partition of the estate before development could go ahead.

Retaining control of the ground rent provided a small income, but also ensured that the terms of the building leases were enforceable. Outright sale risked the loss of control, and the development of anti-social industries or poorly constructed housing that could rapidly deteriorate into slums, and in turn affect the long term yield at the end of the building leases, when the landowner could (in theory) resume control. For those that were prepared to put in their own money, the answer lay in direct development, but only one local landowner, Thomas Courtney Theydon Warner, took this step, and even he sold off isolated parts of the estate.

There were also those who were ready to take advantage of land sales. Ebenezer Clarke jnr was a developer, but he was also a nonconformist who believed in improving housing conditions for locals and migrating Londoners. In 1853-4 he built three cottages at one end of Summit Road (later nos. 2-6 and now demolished), which were offered at reduced rent to poorer people. Clarke obtained a reduction in rates, and met the bulk of these costs himself, rather than pass it on to the tenants. With his fellow director in the Land, Building, Investment and Cottage Improvement Society, Benjamin Rowbotham, he also bought ten plots just off Eden Road in 1862 and put eighteen semi-detached cottages 'for the labouring poor', which became Eden Grove. Clarke's own watercolour (*ill. 91*), complete with picket fencing, rustic trellis work and flowering beds present a sense of space and rural tranquillity that omits the reality of the limited plot sizes, while the later development of the area gives a more crowded feel to the house, but their survival is a testimony to the quality and vision of the man. Clarke became the first chairman of the Local Board in 1873 and produced his own history and directory of Walthamstow in 1861. His commitment to self help was such that at the end of his history, he pledges himself to be available at his house in Grosvenor Park Road between 7pm and 9pm to provide free advice for all comers.

The most common background of those who bought into the new estates was not surprisingly from the land – surveyors, auctioneers, estate agents and solicitors. Pre-eminent among them were the Houghton family. William Houghton was the well placed incomer, seeing business opportunities. Originally a solicitor with offices in the City, who had moved to Walthamstow in 1838 his was the only practice in Walthamstow in 1861. Houghton used his local knowledge– from his clients, as vestry clerk, and as clerk to the local charities and to newly created bodies

91. Ebenezer Clarke's cottages, Eden Grove. Colour print c.1861

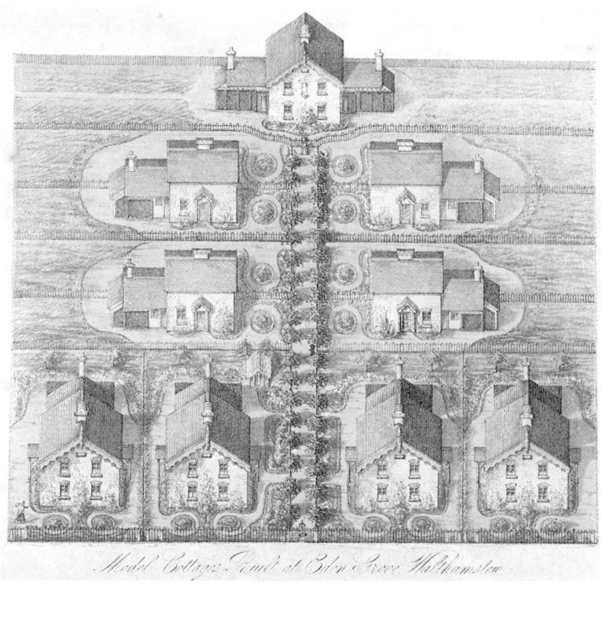

like the burial board to good effect, and to expand on his good works. One son, Gilbert, joined him in the practice and his other, William, became a local auctioneer and between them the family was involved in the development of six estates between 1879 and 1901, with many others passing through their hands via conveyances, and the sale room. We have encountered the Houghtons at home earlier, andwill see them active in local government towards the end of this one.

But there was also a balance to be struck between the aspirations of the landowner, developer and builder, the local characteristics of the area, and what the market would bear. The development of the St James Street area from the 1840s produced small tightly packed houses, and the building of the Walthamstow brewery in 1859 confirmed that future construction would have to be at the poorer end of things. Clarke's vision of rural improvements – "those who remember Whipps Cross will call to mind the little wooden house kept by Mr Southgate as a post office, with a well by the side of the road, and a carpenter's yard. These have now been replaced by a neat row of houses and shops" – was to be offset by suburban squalor in other parts of the parish.

Of course the developer could try for something better. Houghton built houses for rent on the Cedars estate south of Hoe Street station with nothing cheaper than £22 pa. Adjoining estates were renting for £16 pa and as a result the take up on the Cedars estate was very slow. Conversely the Tower Hamlets Building Society had the house size right, but had a poor road layout and inadequate drains, and so although the estate was laid out by 1854 development proceeded slowly and the value of plots dropped. Four plots and two houses sold in 1865 for £410 were only worth £300 at a second sale a mere ten years later. Conversely today, the different periods of building on the Tower Hamlets roads has provided variety through muddle, and which luckily have escaped redevelopment.

STATE OF THE ROADS

It was the state of the newly built roads that provided a regular head of indignation that burst upon the letter columns of the local press. Selborne Road was denounced as a "quagmire and slough of despond". One correspondent to the *Walthamstow Guardian* in 1885 thought

> There are several roads not far from St James-street station which are like ponds of mud and water instead of English roads and on more than one occasion I have seen carts stuck fast in the mud; and to make matters better [sic] the lamps are so far apart and at times it is so late before they are lighted that it is difficult to see where one is going."

But top marks go to 'E.W.' of Albert Road, for an ingenious solution to the problems of the new householders facing a morass. This counter-blast appeared in the *Guardian* of 14 January 1888:

> Sir - The following colloquy recently took place between two inhabitants of Walthamstow.
>
> A: 'How is it that the road in which you live has been properly made up, while our road is a slough?'
>
> B: ' Oh, a member of the Board lives in our road'
>
> This, Sir ... is a point well worth attention and one to which most of your correspondents do not refer. We all know that many months ago an official paper was sent round to the landlords of all the houses in Albert-road, great pains being taken so that none should be left out. In the cases of vacant houses, this paper was affixed to the door. It fulminated dire penalties against all who failed to mend the road within a month. It had, I think, a picture of a lion and a unicorn on top – the representations of the terror and majesty of the law – and on the whole it was prolix and initiatory as a writ or summons. Nevertheless, unlike the demands for rates, it was merely empty threats. The road is still a quagmire and nobody except the unhappy tenants "seems one penny the worse". The landlords, as is natural, not being children, refuse to be coerced by a picture of a lion and unicorn, and the officials, it seems, merely say to each other in a dimly threatening way, "Very well, then. They shall see. A time *will* come".
>
> Now, sir, the true remedy appears to me to be simple. *Get a member of the Board to live in the road.* The householders would, I feel sure, gladly combine to form a subscription for the purpose of paying a part of his rent; and a far-sighted landlord would, I feel sure, make a large reduction with a view to getting the value of his property raised in the end.

In March 1888 the surveyor to the local board reinforced the point:

> To those who from their earliest years have been accustomed to gravel roads, which are dusty and dirty in summer, soft and sloppy in winter, and which wear down under heavy traffic in an almost incredibly short time, it is difficult to bring home the conviction of the necessity and economy of introducing macadam...

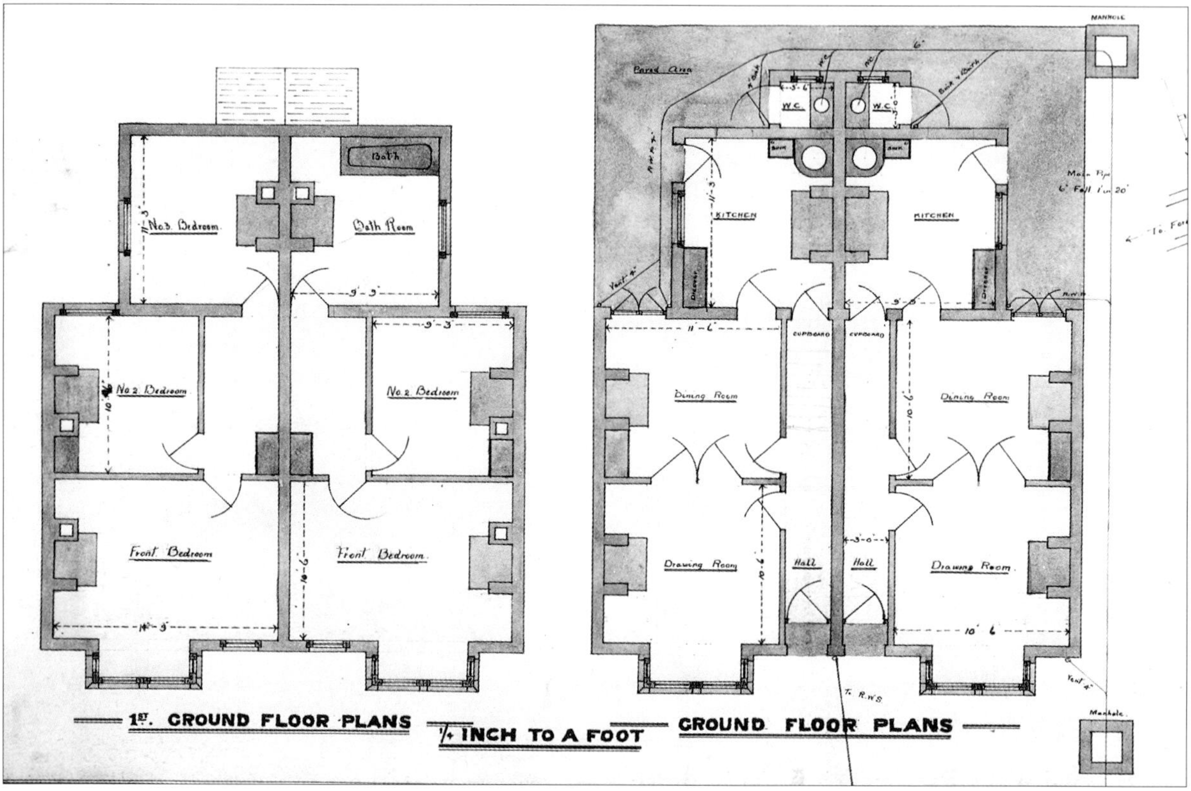

92. Plans for Fern Villas, for Mrs S.A.F. Eason on Brookscroft Road, 1898-9.

Where, the surveyor asked rhetorically, had two thousand cubic yards of gravel spread on the roads over the last six years gone to? In the 1880s Hoe Street had its own crossing sweeper and it was not until later in 1888 that the first local roads – Forest Road and Woodford New Road – were macadamised, and concrete flagstones laid down on the north side of Lea Bridge Road from the junction with Shernhall Street to Whipps Cross.

QUALITY HOUSES?

And then there was the quality of the houses themselves to contend with. Property in the poorer St James Street area tended to be of two types. The cheapest had four rooms for one family or six to seven rooms for two families with an upper storey approached by a separate door - or even a ladder. Larger and slightly better working-class housing provided an additional bedroom. Standards of construction varied. In 1882, Dr Gibbon, the medical officer of health for the Holborn district, informed the Select Committee on Artisans' and Labourers' Dwellings that houses in Walthamstow were built in three weeks, lacked foundations and party walls carried through to the roof, while another local, Thomas Budd, thought that mud had been used instead of mortar, with impending dire consequences.

Some of this was undoubtedly exaggerated but on smaller estates there was little chance of a surveyor being appointed to enforce covenants. Even on larger estates there could be building problems. The Warner estate houses were thoroughly built, but the Prospect Hill estate, aiming at a better class of tenant, were not constructed with the same care. In supporting the creation of the Walthamstow School of Art, Sir Thomas Warner hoped that it would train a better class of builder, who would not emulate the jerry builders of the day.

By the late 1890s houses had slightly more space, but Charles Hodgson's design for C.W. Hodgson's eight-room house at 151 St John's Road

93. Plan and elevation of a house in St John's Road, designed by Charles Hodgson for C.W. Hodgson, May 1898.

still lacked a bathroom and indoor toilet, though there were fittings like the dresser included in the kitchen. However Hodgson's design for the paired Fern Villas on Brookscroft Road for Mrs S.A.F. Eason incorporates a bathroom in one of the pair as an alternative to the third back bedroom. Mrs Eason had particular tastes in bays, and obviously had the resources to insist on an alteration of the design. There were toilets – though outside at the back of the houses. The tenants of the purpose-built one-bedroom flats put up by Hartshorne Brothers in North Bank Road in 1912 were more fortunate – the layout allowed for a tiny toilet with an access from the scullery.

THE WARNER ESTATE

The development of the Warner estate was on the initiative of Sir Thomas Courtney Warner, who inherited his father's estate in 1875 and after an approach from a local builder, decided to tackle developing his estate himself. He took an initial loan of £1000 from his uncle who provided subsequent loans, which were never repaid, as Warner inherited his uncle's estate on the latter's death in 1883. The first part of the Warner estate roads was started in that year, with larger houses in Carisbrook Road and Pretoria Avenue and flats in Leucha, Chewton and Warner roads. The flats included two bedrooms, a parlour, kitchen and scullery and direct access to a rear garden. Streets were wide and tree-lined. Larger three-bedroom houses were built on some roads for larger families. Warner created the Warner Estate Company Ltd, which was registered in 1891, and the company also launched a retail initiative. The District

94. Advertisement for 'half-house flats' on the Warner Estate.

Supply Stores Ltd were based in the Clock House on Pretoria Avenue and gradually expanded to have six branch stores. The venture did not last much beyond 1915 and thereafter Clock House was used as a Co-operative Bakery. By 1900 the company had built up most of Blackhorse Lane between Edward Road and Pretoria Avenue and put up a mixture of shops and houses at the west end of the High Street.

In the 1890 Wood End House was the first of the old houses in the Wood Street and Shernhall Street area to be demolished for building, with Cromer (later Albion), Fairlight (later Parkstone) roads laid out in 1895 and 1898. Woodlands House lost its northern wing in 1892 for Woodlands Road. Wood Street board school replaced Turner and Budd's stables in 1898 and Pamplin's nursery was built over in the same year. To the west the Rectory manor was sold in the late 1890s, and sixty acres of Highams Park were offered for development from 1893. The opening of Blackhorse Road station on the Tottenham & Forest Gate railway in 1894 started to attract industry to Higham Hill. The Warner Company bought the Winns estate in 1898 and developed the area west of Lloyd Park. Further east the Belle Vue estate, comprising another sixty acres was sold in 1899 and Salisbury Hall farm offered for development in 1904.

The later terrace houses of Highams Park are characterised by greater external moulded plaster detail and aimed at a slightly better off market than the properties to the south of Forest Road, which included houses designed for two families as flats. There was one major exception to this, as larger houses were put up on the Rectory manor estate between Howard Road and the Drive, though few of these survive as the area was the subject of compulsory purchase by Walthamstow's Labour council after the war.

One of the earliest pieces of town planning in Walthamstow was the scheme of 1912, when the Warner Company agreed to co-operate with the council in producing a more informal pattern of streets, in contrast to the rigid lines that had been the norm for developers anxious to make the most use of available land. This produced an estate of 300 houses in the area between Billet Road and Pennant Terrace. Some 1,689 acres of land remained undeveloped in 1925.

THE LOCAL BOARD AND ITS PRECURSORS

The rise in building activity increased pressure on roads and local drainage arrangements. Some time before 1845 the vestry had created a highways committee, later designated a highways board, which met at the former workhouse. A nuisance committee of the vestry was formed in 1857 to oversee improvements in drainage and sewerage, including cleansing ditches. Both were combined into one committee in 1862, and employed an inspector, but four years later dissolved on the advice of their clerk that the task was the responsibility of the West Ham poor law guardians. From 1866-8 the guardians were duly appointed as a small committee, which continued with the inspector's post. This body met weekly during 1866, when there was an outbreak of cholera. In 1868 the vestry resumed its powers, though at the same time the south-eastern area of the parish was designated a special drainage district, with its own committee.

Local efforts also extended to lighting. In 1860 the inhabitants of the Church Common formed their own lighting committee and local people in Wood Street followed suit in the following year. If all this sounds ad hoc, then it was. The highways board maintained those dedicated roads and levied a charge on those roads which benefited from new sewers. In the meantime the pace of development – and population – grew. The stimulus of the passing into law of the Public Health Act of 1872 stimulated the sewer committee to recommend to the parish that a constituted urban sanitary authority be formed. Voting on a limited franchise took place and twelve members were elected in September 1873, comprising a mixture of farmers, builders, businessmen and local gentry. Four members of the highways board were among the new members, including Ebenezer Clarke, who became the first chairman.

The new board faced a considerable challenge. The sewerage arrangements that were adequate for a rural parish, were wholly inadequate in the face of a rapidly rising population. Local dissatisfaction rose, and other independent authorities – the Dagenham Commissioners of Sewers and the Lee Conservancy Board – were also able to keep pressure on board members. In 1875 these agencies combined with Leyton Local Board to serve an injunction on Walthamstow from passing sewage into the Dagenham Brook, which forced the board to make proper local provision.

BOARD MEMBERS AND OPERATIONS

Although the board operated as a harmonious whole in its initial period, the election of William Cluff, a wealthy silk merchant, in 1879 was to change that. Even so the board was regarded as something of an oligarchical club prior to the 1890s. Many members lived near to the church and given the size of the community, it would always be likely that many would have been friends or business associates. Initial concerns were over the new sewerage system, though Cluff tended to take a critical view of much of the board's operations. From the 1880s onwards the rise of the Ratepayers' Association led to concerns over the cost of local administration, and later there were to be full scale clashes between Moderates and the more freely spending Progressives.

The rise of the Radicals in the 1890s broke the hold of the ratepayers and opened up debates, but at the cost of highly polarised politics. The Moderates sided with the Houghtons over the issue of the clerk, but there was also the role of the vicar. To some extent this harked back to battles that had been fought locally – and nationally – in the 1850s over the compulsory church rates, finally won in 1868 when church rates were made voluntary. But the vicar also retained substantial influence on other bodies, including

95. A general election scene in 1895, outside the rooms of the Liberal Unionists in Orford Road. Edmund Byrne won.

the school board, and his role was not resolved until after the creation of the urban district council in 1894. The Radicals were able to put forward comprehensive spending plans and introduced better terms for council employees. In 1891 the leading Radical, James Joseph McSheedy, was even able to insist that printing contracts were only awarded to firms that paid trade union wage rates.

McSheedy will be encountered again in education and as a newspaper editor, and was by far the most colourful of the politicians of the period. He was born in 1852 in Tipperary, and trained as a teacher in Cardiff. He was a headmaster in Staybridge in Cheshire and married the headmistress of a neighbouring girls' school. McSheedy was a tireless worker for the Irish National League and was on close terms with all the leading figures including John Stuart Parnell. He travelled extensively for the League, though after one large meeting in Manchester that he presided over ended in uproar and disorder, he took to carrying a revolver for some time for self protection. He took up a post in Hackney as an assistant schoolteacher for the London School Board, and in Hackney a friend, Joseph Blake, suggested that he move to Walthamstow.

Once in Walthamstow McSheedy was welcomed by local Liberals and recruited to the Progressive party, largely from the poorer neighbourhoods round St James Street. His political aspirations were given voice through his newspapers - covered in a later chapter – but his funds were always in a precarious state as a result of successive libel actions – 28 in all.

Initially the board met at Vestry House, but from 1876 moved to the new town hall, built on the front of the public hall in Orford Road. The town hall, enlarged in 1891, survived to become part of the Connaught Hospital and after use by the North East London Polytechnic is now a community centre and nursery. William Houghton, who had served the vestry, also became clerk to the local board on a part-time basis, and despite the efforts of William Cluff and his supporters, the post remained part time when Houghton was succeeded by his son Gilbert in 1879. The Houghtons benefited directly from the status of the post, as they were also able to collect sundry fees and charges. The stranglehold of the Houghtons on local government was to be of considerable concern to the radical opposition in the 1890s.

The board employed a full-time assistant clerk and accountant from 1887 and a part-time professional surveyor from 1874, although the old parochial surveyor continued as inspector of nuisances until 1880, after which he became assistant and road surveyor until 1891. Cluff secured the appointment of a full-time surveyor from 1880, who also took over the duties of the inspector of nuisances. When responsibility for the district's sewerage schemes changed in 1884, the surveyor also became the engineer, and the three roles were not separated until 1886 when a new post of inspector of nuisances was created. The engineer was also responsible for a growing direct labour force, and in 1891 the office was reorganised to facilitate this.

The areas of principal concern were the state of the roads and the quality of building work, but the board did not have the paid staff to tackle either issue adequately. Initially the board avoided taking over private roads, with the result that roads away from the centre of the parish deteriorated in quality. The board members passed model byelaws governing house construction, but these were often ignored and what was built was often not what had been submitted on the original plans. This should be seen against the rising pace of building, with 5,900 houses built in the twenty years from 1871 to 1891, and so perhaps the collapse of four houses in Marsh Street in 1880 should have surprised no-one.

Thereafter the board ordered that no new house could be occupied until it had been certified by the surveyor. The odd prosecution had little effect, and while the new surveyor improved the detection rate, he gradually lost energy. The creation of a separate post of nuisance inspector in 1884 helped a little, since until then the surveyor was doing building control, food and drugs cases. But even then those who broke the byelaws and had a notice served on them, might havet no further action takenagainst them – as the case of Albert Road demonstrated. Even model byelaws have gaps, as the surveyor found in 1887 when he discovered a batch of substandard bricks on a building site. He could prevent their use in that location, but could not prevent the builder moving them elsewhere for use once his back was turned.

Matters came to a head in 1887-8 when notices were served on 31 builders, and following discussions between builders and the board, some small changes were made to the building byelaws. By 1890 the surveyor was beginning to report a rise in the standards of construction.

SEWERS

The legal action of 1875 on the pollution of Dagenham brook prompted the local board to set up their own sewage works when they acquired Low Hall farm in 1875. In the following year tanks were built to hold sewage from Hale End. In 1880 the sewer from the south east was diverted to Low Hall, and five years later the tank arrangements were replaced by pipes to the enlarged Low Hall works. But the new works did not wholly prevent the pollution of the Lea and in 1895 Leyton threatened further legal action. The London County Council system was inadequate to take any further material and so Low Hall works were again modified. Walthamstow was not connected to the London main drainage system until 1928. Domestic rubbish was connected under contract from 1874, and managed directly from 1891, with refuse disposal facilities added to the Low hall site from 1904.

SWIMMING POOLS, LIBRARIES AND PARKS

Low Hall was also the site of Walthamstow's first swimming pool. The board had given thought to a swimming pool for some years, but when chemical precipitation of sewage was abandoned in 1889, the tanks were surplus to requirement. One was cleaned out and set up in a corrugated iron shed, and was a popular attraction for the next two years. Walthamstow did not get purpose-built baths until 1900, when the High Street baths were built alongside the public library. Enlarged in 1923, they were demolished in 1968. The new public library was built on part of the site in the 1980s.

The recreation ground created by the enclosure of Church Common in 1850 was threatened by the construction of the railway in 1869, which bisected the site. Protracted negotiations led to the purchase of an alternative site in Selborne Road by the vestry in 1869, which was handed over to the local board in 1876. A small playground survives on the south side of the railway, which today is asphalted and fenced, the sole surviving remnant of Church Common. The local board was also able to convert the former gravel pits at Higham Hill and Markhouse Common. After the surveyor had exhausted the gravel for road repairs, these were fenced and levelled for recreation. Selborne Road and the two former gravel pits were all given improved layouts in 1906 under a scheme to provide the unemployed with work.

96. The public swimming baths in the High Street, opened in 1900. Watercolour by William Dunfield, the architect, 1896.

97. Inside the swimming baths, c.1900.

The Public Libraries Act of 1892 permitted all local authorities except counties to become library authorities, although expenditure was limited to 1d in the pound rate. This provided the stimulus for the local board to seek to establish a service for Walthamstow. In 1893 they bought a house called Rosebank next to the Selborne Road recreation ground. A reading room, lit by oil lamps was built in the back garden and opened in September 1894. Initially users could only read newspapers and magazines, and it was not until after the room opened that the librarian could make a start on buying books for lending.

FIRE AND BURIAL

The local board also took over the parish fire brigade. Hand drawn manual engines had been housed in a tiny shed next to the National School – the building still survives today, in use as a garage. By 1883 the board's engine keeper was authorised to enlist six firemen, who were paid for attendance at fires, providing they arrived within half an hour of a fire starting. The service expanded in 1887 and a new station was opened in St James Street, with a further one opening on Willow Walk in 1892. The following year the board made the fire brigade voluntary, with financial support from subscriptions, but with the board appointing the officers, approving the rules, paying for the engineer and owning all the equipment. This resulted in the dismissal of all the previously employed firemen. A steam engine was bought in 1895 and a new station on the High Street opposite Storey Road opened in 1895. It was left to the urban district council to resume full control in 1897-8, but it was not until 1906 that the last of the volunteers had been replaced with fully paid up men. The High Street station closed in 1924 when a station on Forest Road replaced it.

More living also meant more dead. Walthamstow formed a burial board in 1870, which inevitably drew on the services of William Houghton as its clerk. Houghton offered the board what he deemed to be a suitable piece of

98. *Walthamstow Fire Brigade c.1910, probably at the High Street fire station.*

land, but when it was felt to be too costly, he was instrumental in beating down the price of a fellow parishioner, James Innes. Innes felt that he had been roughly treated and complained to Houghton in writing, concluding that the clerk was not a gentleman. The eleven-acre site was on the north side of Queens Road and suffered from poor drainage. In the mid 1870s the vicar of St Saviours, W.A. Grantham Robinson, wrote to complain of conducting burials where the coffin was lowered into water and where digging had had to stop above approved levels, because of rising water. Perhaps under the circumstances it was appropriate for board member D.T. Morgan to apologise to his colleagues for missing a board meeting due to unwanted contact with water – in his case not looking where he was going and falling into the Wood Street sewer. Responsibility for the cemetery passed to the urban district council in 1896.

WATER SUPPLY

Water and gas were both provided by private companies. The main supplier of water for the area was the East London Waterworks Company, which obtained powers for the metropolitan Essex area in 1853. The intake was moved from Lea Bridge to the Copper Mills in 1854. Walthamstow received its first ELWC supplies in the early 1860s, with mains being laid to the area round the parish church in 1863. Walthamstow to the north of Forest Road had to rely on springs, wells and rain water until the late 1870s – the Company had offered, but the local board had declined. Higham Hill people could also get their water from the Woodman public house, where the publican had laid on an additional supply for his watercress beds, which was normally more than he needed. At least one estate company was forced to sink artesian wells in the area to ensure supplies to its newly constructed houses.

However not every house in the area had a supply, and it was not until 1876 that the local board decided to compel owners to have a mains connection. Even then the supply was still inadequate, and there were problems for the fire brigade. In the hot summers of the early 1890s the ELWC was unable to meet the level of demand from those houses it did supply, and householders had to rely on reserve cisterns – though a warning was given not to drink water from such a source.

Earlier the problem had been pollution of the supply from the Lea, but from 1886 intakes from higher up the river removed the worst of the problems, and thereafter the issue became the question of constant supply. The construction of one reservoir at the junction of Haggar Lane and Woodford New Road, and a further twelve on Walthamstow marshes gradually improved the quantity of the supply, but it was not until 1911 that the supply was constant to all connected houses, and it was 1914 before all houses in Walthamstow had mains water.

GAS

The supply of gas was an altogether more chequered affair. The first two local companies were the South Essex Gas, Light and Coke Company and Walthamstow Gas, Light and Coke Company, with none other than William Houghton acting as their solicitor, which was launched in 1852. A promotional meeting was held at the Chequers Inn in the same year. The vestry was critical of the disruption that was likely to be

99. Walthamstow cemetery on the day of opening in 1872.

caused by both to local roads. The WGL&CC would have built its holder on Church Common prompting a spot of 'nimbyism':

> None of the gentlemen who figure as trustees would have accepted office had the works been placed near their own residences. They are not of the class who would set their neighbour's house on fire to roast their own eggs.

A curious comparison, best not pursued too closely, considering that gas was the subject of the simile. Both companies had problems with sites and in the end the WGLCC faded away and the SEGL&CC's engineer William Morley Stears abandoned the idea of leasing land on Clay Street from George Collard and settled on a site near Lea Bridge in Leyton. Shortage of funds brought about the demise of the company in 1858, with the County & General Gas Consumers Company taking over, but that concern also failed in 1868. Stephenson Clarke, a local coal merchant, then stepped in, forming the Lea Bridge District Gas Company to take on the assets.

The new company stayed the course, and gradually extended the supply. The greatest periods of growth were from 1895-1900 when there was a 14% increase in take up, and 1900-01, when growth rose to 20%. Gas services cost 3d per week from 1889, and gas stoves could be bought in quarterly instalments – which was a barrier for the weekly paid working class. An exhibition of gas stoves in the Victoria Hall in 1891 boosted rentals, but it was probably the arrival of the pre-payment meters from 1899 and the change in rental arrangements from quarterly to weekly that supported the consumer surge at the end of the century. There were also problems with quality and quantity of gas supply, especially for those at the end of the mains run on Friday and Saturday nights.

The LBDGC was comparatively slow at extending the mains before the end of the 1880s and as a result most houses did not have a gas supply fitted at time of construction – the exception was

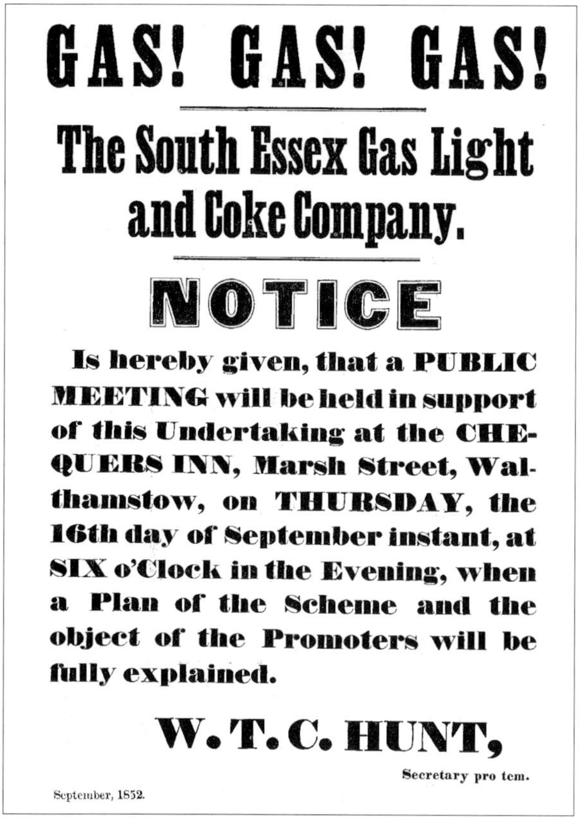

GAS! GAS! GAS!

The South Essex Gas Light and Coke Company.

NOTICE

Is hereby given, that a PUBLIC MEETING will be held in support of this Undertaking at the CHEQUERS INN, Marsh Street, Walthamstow, on THURSDAY, the 16th day of September instant, at SIX o'Clock in the Evening, when a Plan of the Scheme and the object of the Promoters will be fully explained.

W. T. C. HUNT,

Secretary pro tem.

September, 1852.

100. Notice of a meeting seeking support for the plan of the South Essex Gas Light & Coke Company in 1852.

the Prospect Hill estate developed by James Higham in the 1870s. Developers needed a minimum number of suppliers to sign up and this could be difficult with the piecemeal nature of most developments. Gas lamps were also mostly put up by estate owners for the same reason. There had been some early attempts to use sewer gas to supply street lights, but these depended on very secure blow-back valves, and on at least one occasion, there was either no valve fitted or a defective fitting, for one elderly man in the vicinity of Hoe Street was surprised to hear a loud bang, and see a manhole cover surge up into the air, propelled by a burst of flame.

The Lea Bridge District Gas Company remained a small concern. Typical of the gas industry, it introduced a co-partnership scheme for the permanent workforce, partially to act as a barrier to unionisation. It survived until 1948, when it was nationalised.

NEW CHURCHES

The four parish churches created before 1845 met Anglican needs for the next thirty years, but then the growth of population saw the formation of an additional nine parishes before 1909. St Saviour's Markhouse Road, was a Gothic Revival church, built in 1874 and serving a new parish from the following year. One of the patrons was church benefactor Richard Foster and the parish was always high church, with a strong emphasis on ritualism. In this, as in other modern parishes, the inclinations of the founders survived into the 1970s. St Saviour's church became the parish church for the old St James parish, with St James church functioning as a chapel of ease until 1901, when it was demolished and rebuilt. The new church, dedicated to St James the Great, served its own parish from 1904 until 1960, when the church was closed and also demolished.

In the meantime the part of St James parish north of the railway also had its own church built, St Michael and All Angels, Palmerston Road, which was the largest in Walthamstow and was completed in 1885. It became a parish in 1887. St Barnabas, St Barnabas Road, began as a mission of St Saviours, and became a parish in 1901.

St Mary's parish was also divided - St Stephen, Grove Road – a temporary church in 1874 – was replaced by a permanent building in 1878 and became a parish on 1881. St Gabriel, Havant Road began as a mission church, but money for a larger building was never raised. Another mission which met in a laundry in Raglan Road from around 1900 was more successful and St Mark's church was built in 1908, included from 1919 in the parish of St Gabriel. St Mark's church was damaged by bombs in 1941 and destroyed by a V1 in 1944. Flats now stand on the site. St Luke's church, which also began as a mission church, became a parish in 1903, jointly from St Mary and St John – the church dates from the previous year.

In the north St Andrew's was taken from St John's parish in 1908. An iron church went up in 1871, replaced by a permanent church in 1911. Bomb damaged in the last war, it was closed in 1969 and later demolished. All Saints, Selwyn Avenue, was built as a mission of St Peter's Church in Castle Avenue 1898. It became a parish in 1912, when a larger church was built in Selwyn Avenue, though the east end was left incomplete. Lastly St Oswald's, York Road, built in 1909 became a parish in 1924, but lost its church to bombing in 1940. The site was used for flats, built after 1957. St Oswald's ceased to be a parish in 1955.

NEW CHAPELS

102. *The London City Mission in Church Hill Road.*

103. *Folkestone Road Hall. It was rebuilt in 1963.*

The Anglican expansion was also matched by a nonconformist one. The leading nonconformist denomination before 1870 had been the Congregationalists, but they were joined by Baptists and Strict Baptists, Wesleyan and Primitive Methodists. Some churches chose to emulate their congregations and move out of the City. Church Hill Baptist Church is in origin the oldest Baptist Church in London, having begun in Wapping in 1633. By the 1880s the successor church in Commercial Street had lost much of its congregation, with the influx of Jews into the area. It took a further twenty years but the Deacons combined with the Zion Strict Baptist Church in Maynard Road and between them purchased a plot on Church Hill, the site of a number of 'tent missions' in the past. A new church was built there in 1914, which survived into the 1980s, when it was demolished and replaced by a new place of worship combined with flats.

In other cases missionary work by existing churches, later became substantial congregations in their own right, as in Highams Park, where a later Congregational church in Malvern Avenue had its origins in services held in a cottage at Hale End in the 1860s. Some churches were fortunate in being given a helping hand – Spruce Hills Congregational church, founded as a mission with oversight from Trinity Congregational church in 1900, received the gift of a plot of land from John Hitchman, who was a Primitive Methodist, and this enabled the founders to build small and large mission halls. Funding never permitted a permanent church and in the 1930s the larger of the two halls was stripped down and given a pebble-dash rendering. War damage and a diminishing membership led to closure in 1946, though the halls survived in Baptist use until 1963.

Missionary activity led to the foundation of many of Walthamstow's Methodist churches. R.S. Blair was the local founder of Primitive Methodism, when he took a lease of the old Marsh Street New Meeting in 1875. In what had once been regarded as the most aristocratic of the nonconformist places of worship, Blair changed the focus to working with the poor. The church set up missions in Wood Street, on Markhouse common, at Chapel End, Higham Hill and on the Tower Hamlets estate where meetings were held

101. *Wood Street Union Church, 1900.*

in the open air, and again it was with money from John Hitchman given in 1882 that helped get a chapel built in Hawthorne Road, though it had closed by 1917. The best attended of Walthamstow's Methodist churches was the Lighthouse on Markhouse Road, formed in 1888. The permanent church, opened in 1893, owed something of its design, with an angled lighthouse turret, to Captain King of the Bullard line of steamers. The success of the church came in part from the social as well as missionary activities of its members. Founded as a daughter church of Hackney's Pembury Grove church, the Lighthouse did not become part of a Walthamstow circuit until 1941.

There was a wide range of different nonconformist places of worship established in Walthamstow from the 1890s. The Brethren had one of the largest group of supporters in the London area, and from their missions held at the Town Hall in 1884 originated their hall in Queens Road, open by 1886. A hall in Folkestone Road replaced this in 1889, which was rebuilt in 1963 and is now the Potters House Christian Centre. There were other halls in St Andrews Road (1887), Wadham Road (1903), Collingwood Road (1903), and Markhouse Road (South Grove gospel hall, from 1925). The Presbyterian Church of England took over a former Wesleyan chapel on Prospect Hill in 1898, which was rebuilt after bomb damage and finally closed in 1968. The Presbyterian Church of Wales met at Church Hill from 1901 and after some moves bought and demolished Church Hill House in 1932. They converted the stable into a hall, which was in use until they moved to a new church on Leytonstone High Road in 1958. The Salvation Army set up a tent mission in the area in 1888 and built their first citadel on the High Street in 1891, and by 1903 were second only to the Lighthouse in the size of their congregation. The Army bought the Lloyd Park Methodist Church, built in 1914, in 1958, which replaced the High Street citadel by 1961.

Spiritualists have gathered in Walthamstow since 1920, when they held services in a hall next to the Post Office sorting office. In 1924 the group bought the former national school on Vestry Road, and continue to worship there in 2001.

CATHOLICISM

The local Catholic revival began with a Jesuit mission in 1769. In the 1840s mass was being said in local houses, with the support of Jane Sabina Collard, wife of George Collard of Brookfield in Shernhall Street. Jane converted to Catholicism in 1845, and in 1847 persuaded her husband to convey part of Pound Field on Shernhall Street to enable trustees, who included Dr Nicholas Wiseman, to build a school, mission and convent. The mission became St George's Church. In 1848 Jane was asked to convey the remaining part of Pound Field for the school, but she told Wiseman and the priest the Rev. Thomas Doyle, that George Collard would be strongly opposed to the gift. So a complicated substitute was worked out whereby Jane would continue to receive rent from the property as if it was hers for her husband's lifetime. Jane later claimed that this clause would not have force of law and that the property was to be held by three trustees without specifying its final use. Jane consulted her lawyer – William Houghton senior of course – and took the trustees and her own husband to court in 1848.

The case was resolved, and a small stone church opened in 1849 by Wiseman (later to become a Cardinal). However Jane Collard had no intention of being a 'hands off' patron. She has featured in an earlier chapter, and comes across through the documents as strong willed, possessive and difficult to deal with. In the manner of a medieval lord she regarded the church as her own and difficulties developed between her and the new priest Eustace Barron. In 1853 matters came to a head when Jane quarrelled irrevocably with the priest, renounced her faith, revoked all her gifts and locked the church. Wiseman was forced to build a temporary chapel, until St George's could be re-opened in the following year. Full title was not confirmed until the passing of a Chancery decree in 1855.

The original mission church was replaced by a much larger brick building completed in 1901 and dedicated to Our Lady and St George. This burned down on 2 April 1993 and was replaced by the present building, with its impressive curved apse on the north east, which forms the first sight of the church as one rounds the bend of Shernhall Street. The church was dedicated in October 1995. The church of Our Lady of the Rosary and St Patrick opened in Blackhorse Road in 1908 and the church of Christ the King, Chingford Road in 1932.

104. St George's Roman Catholic Church, 2001.

HEALTH CARE

Other than the workhouse, the care of the sick in the nineteenth century was a private matter, though also the subject of charitable support. A dispensary that opened in Orford Road in 1873 was funded by public subscription; it moved to 105 Hoe Street in 1913 and closed in 1942. The former Connaught Hospital in Orford Road began as a voluntary cottage hospital for children in Brandon Road near Wood Street in 1877. From 1880-94 it was in Salisbury Road, but the gift of Holmcroft, a house in Orford Road by local benefactor Alfred Janson in 1894, brought about a move to a site with room for expansion as a children's and general hospital. The hospital had become the Walthamstow, Leyton and Wanstead hospital but was renamed the Connaught in 1928, in honour of its patron since 1894, the duchess of Connaught.

POVERTY AND CHARITY

The reform of the poor law in 1834 brought Walthamstow into the West Ham poor law union and from 1841 all resident paupers from the parishes that comprised the union were moved to the new union workhouse built in Leytonstone. The union had its desired effect, and the cost of maintaining the poor dropped from 60d in the pound to 24d in the pound in three years. However grim the new regime was for those caught up in it, the relief to the ratepayer was palpable. Vestry House was split, with part continuing to be used by the vestry and after 1882 leased to the Literary and Scientific Institute in 1882, and the other going to the police from 1842 to 1870.

From 1880 Vestry House became another part of the charity portfolio. The administration of bequests remained an important part of vestry business. Local charities had been augmented by seven gifts made between 1805 and 1877, with a further four going to support the almshouses, including one from Elizabeth Collard, aunt of George Collard, to the trustees of Squire's

105. *Connaught Hospital.*

Almshouses in 1842. The largest bequest came from Jane Sabina Collard, who after her return to the Anglican fold conveyed a part of the disputed Pound Field and other land to three trustees in 1859 to erect and endow a set of almshouses. One, William Houghton, put up some of his own money to the bequest to bring it to fruition, and the Jane Sabina Collard almshouses, perpetuating the memory of a notable client, went up on Maynard Road in 1881.

The debate over the reorganisation of the Monoux school in the 1870s also prompted the vestry to examine Walthamstow's charities. The dole charities of the previous century were becoming outmoded, when the real demand was for outdoor relief. The initial vigour of the new poor law had been relaxed and by 1878 there were 418 local people collecting relief. Any payments that could come from charitable bequests would cut the burden on the poor rates, which were rising again. The debate about money going to education or to poor relief prompted the vestry meeting on 25 August 1876 to appoint a committee to investigate how the charities were run and to what ends.

The resulting report led to an appeal for an

106. *The Jane Sabina Collard Almshouses.*

enquiry by the Charity Commission, and this sat in the public hall in Orford Road in November and early December 1876. The report, published in 1877 recommended the creation of a new single governing body and the diversion of money to support the reform of Monoux school. Dole charities could be discontinued and trustees from the new body should be local people. But the Commissioners did not recommend compulsion, and the result was only partial reform. The Walthamstow Charity Governors, formed under the Scheme of 1880 comprised the vicar, churchwardens, six governors appointed by the vestry and four co-optive governors chosen initially by the Commission and thereafter by the Charity Commissioners. The WCG took over eleven charities, but the vicar, Thomas Parry feared that Squire's almshouses would be compelled to take in non-Anglicans, against the founder's wishes, and on the same grounds objected to the transfer of Mary Newell's charity, which sponsored apprenticeships for Anglican children. The Jane Sabina Collard almshouses also remained outside the scheme.

The new governors comprised those who would soon be seen as the parish oligarchy – men like

107. David Thomas Morgan, 1885.

108. John Francis Holcombe Read.

Ebenezer Clarke, David Thomas Morgan, John Francis Holcombe Read and William Elliot Whittingham had all served on the vestry or on the local board – or both. Naturally the new governors turned to that local fountain head of knowledge – and fees, and appointed William Houghton as their clerk. Despite his opposition to the principle of amalgamation, Thomas Parry became chairman of the governors.

The reforms left four sets of charity trustees, for besides the WGC, Houghton and his fellows for Jane Sabina Collard almshouses, and the vicar for Squire's almshouses and two related charities, the churchwardens continued to control a further ten charities, and a share in the Maynard charity. Four became three with the death of Parry in 1892, as his successor William Langthorne transferred his charities to the WGC. The mul-

109. *William Elliot Whittingham.*

tiplicity of bodies allowed radical political James Joseph McSheedy to make the charities a target, claiming poor administration and bias in favour of Anglicans. Charities were something of a test case for the wider issues raised by the Radicals of greater public accountability.

OPEN LOCAL GOVERNMENT

The battle began in April 1890, when McSheedy, as an elected vestryman, proposed a committee, chaired by himself, to examine the accounts of the charities and report back. The resulting report was presented at a vestry meeting that ran over three nights in July 1891 and was then widely circulated. Uproar resulted from McSheedy's allegations that £4,000 had been diverted from the poor to build Monoux school and that Houghton had benefited unduly through his sundry offices at the expense of the poor.

It is worth just recapping just what a pluralist William Houghton had become. He was Clerk to the vestry, Clerk to the Churchwardens, Clerk to the Burial Board, Clerk to the Local Board, Clerk to the Walthamstow Charity Governors, Clerk to the Monoux school Governors and Trustee and

110. *Mr and Mrs Young ran a soup kitchen in premises behind the Chequers Inn on the High Street. Deserving children clutch bread and cans of hot soup. Photograph c.1900.*

Walthamstow Electors!

Read this, and VOTE TO-DAY.

Carefully Examine these Two Pictures.

What the Progressives have done. 1897—1900.	What the Pro-Chinese have done. 1901—1904.
Provided— Splendid Public Baths. A Charming Park. Well-built Isolation Hospital. Successful Electric Lighting, which has produced £3,000 profit this year, equal to a 2d. Rate. An excellent Technical Institute. Manufacture of Concrete Paving, which has made £3,000 profit this year, equal to a 2d. Rate.	**Nothing!** But squandered the £6,000 profit.

111. Part of an election address on behalf of the Progressive Party in the local elections in 1904. The Conservatives had supported the use of immigrant Chinese labour into the British Empire. The label 'pro-Chinese' was therefore attached to the 'Moderates' – the local version of the Conservatives.

Clerk to the Jane Sabina Collard Charity. McSheedy sought to have Houghton sacked as vestry clerk, but the October 1891 meeting called for the purpose descended into chaos. In an atmosphere of pamphlet and counter-pamphlet, a public poll was called, in which 2,340 ratepayers voted, giving Houghton a substantial majority of 702 votes. For whatever reason those who paid the bills were with the oligarchs.

The running battle continued through the summer of 1892. At one meeting, the police were called in, as the *Walthamstow Guardian* reported in its issue of 23 August. McSheedy had just handed his resolution to the chairman, vicar William Langthorne,

> who ignored it and it was taken possession of by Mr Houghton, who, gripping Mr McSheedy tightly round the body, pressed him towards the edge of the platform ... a member of the audience ... rushed to Mr Houghton's assistance and, getting hold of Mr McSheedy, threw him almost headlong along the excited audience near the platform. In falling, Mr McSheedy described a parabolic curve, but though his fall was broken by ... being caught by a member of the audience, he was considerably mauled in the melee that ensued. For some moments there was a wild struggle in which fists and sticks were freely used, but in the end Mr McSheedy, minus his spectacles and part of his neck tie, remounted the platform among yells and cheers. When he did so, the Vicar was leaning over the table smiling and tightly grasping the minute and account books, Mr W. Houghton had disappeared and the Vicar proceeded to business by saying, 'Mr Churchwarden Knott will now read the minutes of the last meeting ....

In the end McSheedy got the Charity Commission enquiry he had been seeking, and while no wrong doing was proved, the WCG and the churchwardens accepted the need for a new scheme. This was strengthened when the Collard trustees joined the proposal in April 1894 and a revised scheme of October 1895 created the Walthamstow Parochial Charities. In future ten trustees would be appointed, two by the Guardians of the Poor Law Union and eight by the new urban district council, two from each of the new eight wards. Four additional trustees would be co-opted by the Charity Commission initially and then by the other trustees. In the spirit of compromise the vicar remained an ex-officio trustee.

The new scheme was part of changes in local government. Under the Local Government Act of 1894, the local board was abolished and gave way to the Walthamstow Urban District Council in 1895. Eighteen members represented four wards, among whom was McSheedy, sitting as a St James Ward member. The new council took over the functions of the burial board, became a constituted electrical authority in 1895 and the

112. Down but not out. J.J. McSheedy as seen in the pages of an opposition paper, the Walthamstow and Leyton Herald, 5 May, 1899.

elementary education authority in 1903. As we have seen it also ventured into municipal tramways. The Progressives, led by McSheedy flexed their muscles from the start, and in 1894 McSheedy opposed the appointment of W.T. Herbert as the first librarian. Herbert was the son of Samuel Herbert, controlling editor of the *Guardian* and when McSheedy's constant attacks succeeded in getting Herbert jnr to resign in 1895, the vituperation of the *Guardian* reporting of Progressive activity knew no bounds, affecting the first period of Progressive control, from 1897-1901.

Although the council swung between Moderates and Progressives, Labour and Socialist candidates were coming forward, though with little support at first. The first Labour success was the election of H. Bird to the School Board in 1900 (the candidate or his supporters had a sense of humour, for a later election card urged the electorate to 'Plump for Bird'). And there were other changes – the retirement of Gilbert Houghton in 1895 saw the creation of a full time post of vestry clerk and signalled the end of the Houghton period of pluralism. Some things did not alter so quickly. The Progressive majority from 1897 was small and bickerings were frequent and the odd fight unremarkable in the council chamber. Charges of overspending brought down the first Progressive administration, though it had also coincided with the peak of building development, for in the five years of 1898 to 1902, 8,800 building applications were passed. The costs of McSheedy's libel actions and the failure of his newspaper caught up with him and he left the council in 1904, ending his days as a respectable headmaster of Winns Avenue School, dying in 1923.

But for a while Walthamstow had its own special place in the lexicon of local politics. Let the *Daily Graphic* of 4 November 1902 have the last word on an unequalled period of turbulence:

> Those who like their politics hot should go to Walthamstow... Roughly speaking their elements are divided into McSheedyism and anti-McSheedyism. There are traces of a third policy known as Constitutional Progression, but it is not quite certain where this comes in. It matters little however to the aspiring politician. He may label himself with the badge of any party with equal certainty of an opportunity of committing an assault or of himself being assaulted. For in this deliberative assembly they have rough and ready methods of dealing with inconvenient minorities. Members are liable to be called to order by a blow on the head from the chairman's mallet, and a debate may be concluded by the knocking out of teeth.

113. Monoux School and almshouses in 1915.

Learning for life

MONOUX'S SCHOOL

Walthamstow owes its first school to George Monoux, as just one of the benefactions he made to his adopted parish. The land he purchased from Christchurch Priory in 1527 was intended for the construction of almshouses "and the edification and building for a schole master and a ffree schole...." Monoux was careful to specify the size of the schoolmaster's apartments in the building and indicated that the master should be of quiet and honest disposition, prepared to pray for the souls of Monoux and his family. But beyond defining the intake as being between twenty and thirty pupils, unless the master wished to teach more, the founder gave no indication as to what should be taught. He did not stipulate that the school should be a grammar school, mindful perhaps that a school serving around the 450 or so who lived in early 16th century Walthamstow would need to provide a more general education.

Monoux died in 1544, leaving property in the City of London to fund the school and the almshouse. For the next two hundred and forty years the school was administered along with the rest of Monoux' bequest, by trustees of variable quality (*see pp 102-107*). Relatively little is recorded of the school's first hundred years. When the chantry, of which the almshouse and school formed a part, was abolished in 1548, the visiting commission recorded that the school master, John Hogeson, a cleric aged 40 was "of goode usage and conversacion, litterate and teachithe a schole". The first of the charitable Inquisitions into the Alford's handling of the Monoux charity touched on the quality of the master, noting that in the past one master had been appointed who had been unable to teach Latin. The money paid to secure the place of master would have had to be recouped by the successful candidates through fee paying pupils.

The Commission of 1659 established that the future masters were to be graduates, and effectively confirmed the status of grammar school and it seems from the lack of records that the school continued with a mixture of free and fee

114. *Interior of Monoux School in 1915.*

paying pupils. This was the position in 1781 when Walthamstow Vestry appointed a committee to negotiate with the Monoux trustees to purchase their parts of the church. The Monoux trustees also sought to divest themselves of the running of the school and this became part of the final bargain that had no basis in law. The schoolmaster of the time, Rev. Griffith Lloyd, had to be compensated and was granted a lifetime annuity of £20, while retaining his accommodation in the almshouse building, where he also lodged his boarders. The free school consisted of eight pupils, taught by a separate schoolmaster employed by Lloyd. The free pupils were not taught Latin by their own schoolmaster but could have lessons either from Lloyd or from a visiting schoolmaster. This kind of dual status school was by no means uncommon at the time – Chigwell School was run on similar lines.

BLUE, GREEN AND GREY SCHOOLS

However Lloyd died before the trustees relinquished control and the senior churchwarden, Joel Johnson had to make provision for the pupils until a new master was found. The school rules were revised and the intake rose to thirty boys and twenty girls. Johnson provided a school uniform and Monoux school became known locally as the Blue School, distinguishing it from the Green School. This was Marsh Street British School, established by local nonconformists in 1789 supposedly as the result of derogatory remarks made by the Monoux schoolmaster about their children in his charge. By 1818 there were twenty girls. Mrs Elizabeth Solly, from the nonconformist family with links to Eliezar Cogan and the Old Meeting House in Marsh Street, is said to have been the founder of the Grey School of Industry, which had 19 pupils in 1807. The school was still in operation then, but probably mirrored the declining fortunes of the Old Meeting House, whose congregation dwindled and which closed in 1835. Lady Wigram of Walthamstow House was also running a short lived charity school in 1807 when there were twelve children, but it had closed before 1818.

Bills for Blue School uniforms for 1815 survive. The boys' suits were made from dyed kersey. The girls gowns were made from 'Superfine Long Ells', made into gowns and petticoats with linings and trimmings.

The poorest children were those who lived in the workhouse. In 1741 the parish employed an eighty-year-old widow to teach sewing and reading. In 1777 two school mistresses were employed to teach the children "to read and write and cast accounts one hour every morning and every afternoon and catechised every other day and say Lord's Prayer and belief every morning and night." One room was used as the schoolroom, for in 1818 the privy in it was repaired! In 1807 ten children were taught at the school

PRIVATE SCHOOLS

One of the earliest of Walthamstow's private schools was opened by Robert MacFarlane at Shern Lodge from about 1770 to around 1795. Early nineteenth-century Walthamstow had a number of private schools. Eliezar Cogan came to Walthamstow as minister of the Old Meeting in Marsh Street in 1801. In his previous positions at Ware, Enfield and Cheshunt, he had run a school, and at the end of 1801 when he moved to Essex Hall, he also brought his school to Walthamstow, using the coach house as the schoolroom. He continued with his teaching after retiring from the ministry in 1816, and his pupils included Benjamin Disraeli, who became leader of the Conservative Party and Prime Minister, Russell Gurney, QC and Recorder of London, Samuel Lister, an eminent surgeon, and W.E. Nightingale, the father of Florence Nightingale. Old age brought about the closure of the school in 1828, when Cogan's former pupils subscribed to a painting as a token of their affection. Cogan died in 1855, and is buried in the New Gravel Pit burial ground in Chatham Place, Hackney.

In 1820 the five private schools in Walthamstow included Paradise House Academy at Whipps Cross, which housed 94 pupils, mostly boys in 1811, and Miss Caley's school, in a house on the site of Palace Parade on the High Street. After 1815 this lay behind Wragg's coaching house. From 1814 to 1818 Fanny Keats, sister of the poet, went to school here, walking up the road from her guardian's house, the Elms. John Coe, also vestry clerk, built his own school in Wyatts Lane in 1820.

115. Eliezar Cogan.

NATIONAL SCHOOLS

By 1818 the Blue School had 60 pupils, but in September of that year the Vestry was told that complaints had been received about disorder in the girls school. The mistress was sacked and her replacement worked under the scheme laid down by the National Education Society. The old premises were also becoming overcrowded and a new school was built, funded by voluntary subscription, on the other side of the common from the workhouse. The new National School building was originally intended to house the girls' school, the Sunday school and the girls from the workhouse, but in addition it was also decided to move the boys in as well, and the new building had to contain two hundred pupils when it opened in 1819. It was enlarged a mere six years later in 1825.

THE INFANT SCHOOL

Some two years after his arrival as the new vicar of Walthamstow in 1822, William Wilson was finally persuaded by his brother to visit a new experimental school for infants in Spitalfields, established in 1820 by Samuel Wilderspin. Wilson was won over to the new school and invited Wilderspin to see if a similar establishment would

116. St Mary's Infants' School. Engraving by M.R. Giberne.

work in a rural parish where the children would have farther to travel to school. Wilson had chosen to live in a house on Grove Street, whose extensive grounds lay between Beulah Path and Beulah Road, with a garden of over 340 feet stretching back almost to Maynard Road. He allowed Wilderspin to use an old barn in his grounds and after five weeks of labour by Wilderspin, his daughter and a teacher from the Spitalfields school, the new infant school opened in 1825. The school was so successful that Wilson wrote up the experiment in a book that went through three editions within twelve months of its publication in 1824. Wilson went on to launch the construction of one of the first purpose built infant schools in the country, built on a piece of former glebe land to the west of the churchyard. Walthamstow Infant School opened in 1828. The present entrance alongside Squire's Almshouses was a later addition, taken from the churchyard. Restored in 1928, the infant school served local children until it closed in 1978 and is now the Welcome Centre, available for community use.

MONOUX SCHOOL AFTER 1820

The Monoux school had remained above the almshouse after the foundation of the National school, and after a short-lived appointment, the parish took on J.F. Roberts in 1820. Roberts changed the curriculum, and rented the Walnuts, next to the churchyard, with capacity for up to thirty boarders, who provided the bulk of his income. Edward Berthon, son of a London merchant with Walthamstow connections, left his impression of life at the school at the time. He arrived at the school aged 9 in 1820 and recalled the poor food and variable quality of the teaching – but he survived the regime to go on to Cambridge. By Berthon's time the old schoolroom had seen better days and he remembered it as "a wretched draughty loft with a steep open tiled roof". A joint of salted beef served on Saturday with potatoes and 'pudding' was served up cold throughout the week for the mid day meal, supplemented by stale bread, milk and water morning and evening. In the end the boys smashed the crockery washing bowls and jugs in their rooms in protest. Roberts – ' Old Bob'– threatened wholesale flogging, but deterred by the size of some his oldest pupils reduced the threat to drawing lots, with the two losers getting the beating. Berthon and his cousin Ben were the last to draw and would have been flogged if Roberts had not had second thoughts.

In the end Roberts' excessive attention to his boarders at the expense of the day school led to his dismissal by the parish in 1836. His successor appointed a deputy, who took on the majority of the teaching, especially after 1842 when the masters were required by the vicar to take on the religious duties specified in Monoux's will that had fallen into abeyance – effectively becoming curates rather than teachers. By 1848 some teaching was in the hands of another clergyman, Dr Greig of Walthamstow House, though with the prohibition on taking boarders around the 1840s, school numbers sank to around 25 pupils – or fewer. From the early 1850s to 1889 teaching was in the hands of Henry Griggs, who did his best with the deteriorating schoolroom. One pupil of the early 1860s recalled that the cracks in the floorboards offered the boys the entertainment of pouring water down on to the heads of the luckless almsfolk below – clearly one instance when young and old should not have mixed.

But there were other problems. Griggs was not a graduate, as required by the revised scheme of management, the school was no longer free and

117. *Forest School. Watercolour by T. Stuart Milner, 1934.*

the results were poor. Higher elementary education could be had at the National School. The solution could have been to expand the teaching staff, but there could be no money from boarders and the funds from the charity were too low.

FOREST SCHOOL

There were also competing schools. In 1830 Archibald du Boulay set up Exeter House school, with a strong scientific element to his curriculum in a house in Forest Place. This lasted only three years, but in 1834 a committee of twelve refounded it as the Forest Proprietary School, intended for the sons of gentry and the teaching of classics, modern languages and science. Opening with three masters and 22 boys, the new school had its own library by 1836 and was able to use the adjacent St Peter's in the Forest church after it was consecrated in 1840 in lieu of a school chapel. By then there were eighty boys at the school.

But the Proprietary school also faced problems in the 1840s. Costs rose, numbers of pupils fell and there were complaints of neglect and incidents of brutality – one boy was struck over the head several times with a heavy book. The son of a proprietor fell through the ice of an adjoining pond and was drowned. The school was on the verge of closure when the head master left. J.F. Boyes, who became head in 1844 determined the school would survive. He took a cut in salary, sacked the more brutal of the staff and four years on handed over to John Gilderdale. Gilderdale bought out the other proprietors and under his ownership the school name was shortened to Forest School. His successor from 1857, F.B. Guy, had been a private tutor to William Morris in 1851-2. The school link with Morris was commemorated in a later commission by the school to Morris' firm for a window in the south transept of the chapel, designed by Burne Jones, which was a casualty of bombing in 1944. A Morris tapestry was also bought to hang in the dining hall. Guy retired in 1886, to be succeeded by his brother, and the Guy family remained owners until 1935. The school survived the destruction of the Junior school in 1944, and post war expansion included the opening of a girls' school in 1981.

NATIONAL AND BRITISH SCHOOLS

As the population grew, Anglicans and nonconformists expanded existing schools and built new ones. St John's National School at Chapel End opened in 1835. In 1839 a new British School for boys and girls was built behind the Marsh Street New Meeting House and absorbed the old Green School and a smaller British school linked to Wood Street Independent Church. This was funded by subscription and chapel donations until it received a government grant around 1877, though five years earlier it had moved to a new building with 173 places in Marsh Street, opposite Buxton Road. Hale End National school for infants opened *c.*1835 and there was also an Anglican school for St James parish from 1842, replaced by a new building on Markhouse Road in 1874, which became St Saviour's school in 1875 with the creation of the new parish. A British school at Shernhall Street was linked to Wood Street Congregational Church and was the ancestor of Wood Street British School. It was grant aided in 1868 and moved to new premises on Shernhall Street in 1872. A British school at Higham Hill existed in 1870 in a building belonging to the Society of Friends and formed the basis of a later Board school.

St George's Roman Catholic School was founded in 1850, with support from the catholic Poor School Committee, initially in Shernhall Place (later RaglanRoad). By 1887 there were 51 pupils.

WALTHAMSTOW SCHOOL BOARD

But the combined efforts of local religious bodies were not enough to keep pace with the growing population of the district in the 1870s and in 1880 the Government's Education Department stepped in to force the formation of a local school board, whose initial instruction was to create places for an additional 950 children. Nonconformist schools accepted the offer of the new Walthamstow School Board to take them over, but Anglicans stayed independent. In the next 23 years the Board built thirteen permanent and two temporary schools, providing 16,150 places. It also created two special schools, a part-time pupil teacher centre and evening class instruction. Three further new schools planned by the Board were completed by its successor, the Walthamstow Education Committee in 1903-6.

The school board also made good use of new legislation on provision for children with disabilities. In 1893 it took a census of local blind and deaf children and in 1900 opened the William Morris school for the deaf at Queens Road followed three years later by one for children with learning difficulties in Pretoria Avenue. After the demise of the school board, the Urban District Council opened the Joseph Clarke school for the blind in 1918 in Gainsford Road and centre at Joseph Barrett school for children with physical disabilities in 1924. This also used part of Brookfield orthopaedic hospital and after moving to Hale End in 1936 became the Hale End open air school.

Just as Walthamstow had been early in the field of schools for infants, it also saw the creation of one of the earliest nursery schools in the country, on Low Hall Lane in 1929.

118. The Laundry Centre at Queens Road Board School, c.1900.

119. The Cookery Centre at the Wood Street Board School, c.1900.

TRANSFORMING MONOUX SCHOOL

The 1880s also saw changes and reform to secondary school education. The Monoux School was ripe for reform when in 1870 three factors seemed to provide an opportunity for action. A new curate refused to accept the additional duties of the almspriest-schoolmaster. The school had been viewed in 1866 by an inspector from the Schools Enquiry Commission and his report, presented to the House of Commons, was critical of Henry Griggs the master and of the low standards he achieved. Thirdly, under the Endowed Schools Act of 1869 the trustees could augment the endowment of such schools from other charitable sources, such as apprenticeship schemes, and dole charities, which by the mid Victorian period were under-used.

But a draft scheme to convert the school into a middle class establishment, published in 1873, failed, as the governors of charities scheduled for the support of the school could not agree the terms, and there was opposition in the wider community, including from the Working Men's Institute, one of whose officers was Griggs. He understandably feared being pensioned off, since the master of the reformed school would have had to be a graduate. A new attempt in 1877 also stalled, but then late in 1879 Griggs died. A temporary master may have been engaged but the school had closed entirely by January 1881. Three years elapsed before the Charity Commissioners published a scheme to re-found the school, diverting money from two other parochial charities.

The new school reopened in 1886 in a schoolroom in West Avenue, hired from Trinity Congregational Church. The new headmaster, Henry Allpass was later to combine his work with a curacy of St James Parish and was to teach not less than two hundred pupils aged from seven to fifteen. The curriculum included Latin, one modern language, science, and vocal music besides the mainstays of the three 'r's, geography, history and non-denominational religion. After three and a half years the school moved to a new building on High Street, which opened in December 1889. Allpass placed the school on firm ground and while the school song composed by local music enthusiast and school governor, J.F.H. Read, might have overstated the case when it proclaimed the school as a 'monument of fame', Monoux School rapidly gained an important place in the pantheon of local learning.

The finances were harder to get right. More charitable income was diverted in 1890, and this was the subject of local opposition, becoming one of the *causes célèbre* of Radical politician J.J. McSheedy. The claims of mismanagement and

120. The Monoux School as rebuilt at Chapel End in 1927.

dishonesty may have been over stated, but McSheedy was able to tap into strong local feeling that money intended for the poor ought not to be diverted for the benefit of the middle class. However the school fees, at £6 pa for older boys and an additional £2 for books were just within range of the better off artisans, who wanted their sons to enter the professions, the Civil Service or the City as clerks. There was always the chance of a scholarship, but only six or seven of these were available out of the annual intake of around 45 pupils.

SECONDARY AND TECHNICAL EDUCATION

1890 also saw the foundation of Walthamstow's first secondary school for girls. What was to become the Walthamstow county high school for girls began as a private school run by a committee of subscribers, in the Trinity schoolroom recently vacated by the Monoux Grammar School. But it rapidly found a better home in Church Hill House after a few months. There were 108 girls and four boys at the school in 1906. The take over by the county council in 1911 led to a move to new premises on the old vicarage glebe in 1913. Later enlargements have taken in the Victorian vicarage itself, which has been retained for school use.

Reform at Monoux was also accompanied by improvements in technical education. The Walthamstow Literary and Scientific Institute founded a school of art in 1883, which also used that cradle of local education, the Trinity schoolroom in West Avenue. Run by the Science and Art Department at South Kensington, it moved to Grosvenor House, Hoe Street in 1892 and then to Court House on the other side of the road in 1900. Michael Sadler's report on secondary education in Essex published in 1906, praised the strong artistic tradition. In 1891 Walthamstow formed a technical instruction committee, which received grants from the county council, which it passed on to the school board and the art school. A technical institute and day school was founded at Grosvenor House in 1897 and there were 700 students in 1906. The art school passed under the control of Walthamstow's Education Committee in 1906, but closed in 1915.

Among the private schools founded after 1850 was the Walthamstow school of shorthand and typewriting, which began in 1895. Renamed in 1933 as Walthamstow Business College it closed in 1957, though a painted advert lingers on at the end of a house in Stainforth Road. Clark's College, opened a branch at Cleveland House in 1913 – a branch already existed at Clapton Common – which lasted until 1966.

SPLITTING RESPONSIBILITY

The Education Act of 1902 split the responsibility for education, with the county taking over secondary and Walthamstow Urban District Council running elementary schools. The UDC built six new schools between 1907 and 1929 and a further four in the next ten years. Two new Roman Catholic schools were built in 1930-1.

Monoux school faced two reports in 1906, one which criticised the over emphasis on scientific subjects– although this was no more than the balance provided in the 1960s. But much of the teaching was seen as outmoded and unimaginative. In 1907 the Board of Education threatened to withdraw its recognition of efficiency from the school, effectively pressurising Essex County Council to fund an additional master. However if there concerns about teaching standards, the school had developed a lively tradition of sport and concerts, and the annual prize giving took place at the Victoria Hall in Hoe Street. The school inspired loyalty, evinced by the formation of an Old Boys' Club, and formed the beginning of social contacts that would prove useful in later life for many pupils.

A further inspection of 1913 was also highly critical and again threatened withdrawal of recognition, which would have led to the loss of half the school's income. The only solution seemed to lie in a take over by the County Council and this was in train in the autumn of 1914 when the headmaster, who had been the main target of the criticism, died suddenly. The threat was lifted and instead a merger between the Monoux school and the former technical school at Grosvenor House, which had become the Walthamstow High School for Boys, was effected in 1916. A new site for the enlarged school on fields alongside Chingford Road was already planned, but a dispute delayed the move and it was not until July 1927 that the school moved to its new buildings. In the intervening years the High Street site became increasingly crowded within and surrounded by the bustling street market without. Gillards pickle and pie factory lay directly opposite on the north side of the High Street, perhaps providing the excuse for a generation of masters to put many pounds of Rough Shag tobacco to good effect in the staff room, producing what one master remembered as "a kind of warm fug... conducive to the telling of exceptional stories ..." . Like as not it was bought from the headmaster, one of whose few perks was a licence to sell tobacco to his assistant masters.

After the county council had assumed control of higher education, it opened a trade and engineering school for boys in Grosvenor House in 1917, joined two years later by a commercial and trade school for girls at the Chestnuts, Hoe Street. In 1938 both were combined to become part of South West Essex technical college, which also included Leyton's technical colleges and the Leyton school of art. A new building on Forest Road designed by J. Stuart, opened in 1939, though the number of students compelled the college to retain Grosvenor House (until it was destroyed in a fire in 1945) and the Chestnuts for evening classes and overflow. In 1957 the technical school moved to Billet Road and became the McEntee county technical school, named after a Walthamstow politician. One of the teachers at the South West Essex technical collage in the late 1950s was the artist Peter Blake and among his art pupils in 1959 was the 17-year-old Ian Dury. Both left for the Royal College of Art in 1963. Dury went on to a be a singer, songwriter and actor. His group, Kilburn and the Highroads, gave their farewell gig in Walthamstow Assembly Rooms in June 1976, just at the time punk was beginning to get established. The support bands were the Sex Pistols and the Stranglers. *New Boots and Panties*, released in 1977 by Dury's new group, Ian Dury and the Blockheads, included the number *Billericay Dickie*, with its tribute to sundry Essex maidens, but omitting Walthamstow. Something to do with the scansion perhaps.

During the Second World War evacuation closed down some schools temporarily. Many were renamed in 1957, often simply losing the word 'street' from their original names. Five new schools were built in 1957-64. With the formation of the London Borough of Waltham Forest in 1965 plans were put forward for comprehensive education and accepted in 1966, with implementation following in 1968. This resulted in substantial change for the Monoux Grammar School, which dropped the 'grammar' but remained a boys' school. New building included a science block and changes in the curriculum introduced more practical subjects. The charitable link between the school and the parochial charities was broken in 1957, when a new charity scheme came into operation and a single lump sum was paid to the Sir George Monoux Grammar School Foundation. Monoux School's comprehensive period came to an end in 1986, after which it was a sixth form college for seven years and is now an incorporated college.

Shops, Shows and Self-Help

NINETEENTH-CENTURY SHOPPING

There was no local market in Walthamstow until the early 1880s, so before then the local shopkeepers bought their produce, notably dairy goods and poultry from the long established markets at Brentwood, Epping, Romford and Waltham Abbey. The gentry would have bought their finer goods in London, but there were small shops and family firms serving local needs. One such was Turner and Budd. William Turner had been living in a house on the corner of Wood Street and Wyatts Lane from 1813. In 1831 he set up a grocer's and corn merchant's business with his near neighbour John Budd, taking two houses on the site of Woodside School. Their premises had extensive stabling at the rear for taking orders from the large houses in the morning and delivering in the afternoon. Vans also made daily trips to London for supplies. As was common in larger businesses shop assistants lived in. Women would lose their place on marriage, though one had a special leaving present, when an older colleague made her a paper model of the shop she was about to leave. The partnership ended in 1860, after which John Budd carried on alone, also serving the parish as overseer of the poor from 1838-9 and three stints as churchwarden, the last from 1865-7. He died in 1868 and his son took advantage of the coming of the railway to expand, building a new warehouse just north of the station in 1877 for the grocery and corn chandler's, while the old premises became a grocer's and wine merchant's. Budd survived the departure of their gentry customers and sold out to another grocer in 1897.

Gilbert Houghton, recalling the Wood Street of his youth in the 1860s listed the local shops. North of Jeffreys Square and the Duke's Head were a baker, a coach maker, a butcher, and then beyond Turner and Budd's premises the post office, which additionally was a sweetshop. There was also a chemist and a hairdresser.

One of Wood Street's traditional shops has survived, due entirely to the tree that has shaded it for most of the last century. Jones butcher's shop claims to date from 1750, but is likely to be later. Behind the wooden building was a yard and

121. Turner and Budd's stable yard seen from the window of Houghton's house on the east side of Wood Street and looking towards the junction with the modern Forest Road. Photograph c.1870, from the Houghton album.

122. Frank Ison's corner shop in Orford Road, 2001. The shop front was remodelled by architect Charles Hodgson around the turn of the century and is an increasingly rare example in the area.

slaughterhouse which survived into the 1960s. Sheep and cows from the local area were driven down Wood Street to be held in the pens at the back as late as the 1920s. The original shop had a hinged drop front, with a wooden table outside for serving customers. Later the front was altered and the present window added, with tiling. Meat was hung outside but otherwise not displayed, and there was also a salting tub for the home production of salt beef and silverside. The business closed in the 1970s and efforts to have the shop listed met with no success, since the body then responsible for listing buildings in London would not accept that there remained sufficient of the 'original' fabric left to justify saving it. Luckily the tree preservation order prevented anything being built on the site that would damage the roots, and at the time of writing is a wholefood shop.

The construction of the Chingford branch of the railway provided the stimulus that gradually changed the character of Marsh Street, as the larger houses and local estates were developed. In 1861, when the population stood at 7144, the main shopping streets were Wood Street (and Whipps Cross) and Marsh Street, but with smaller shopping areas at Church End, and Orford Road. There were no less than 27 boot and shoe makers, some operating from cottage property in back streets, and nineteen grocers, almost all south of Forest Road. Marsh Street was still a sleepy backwater and when trade was slow, the shopkeepers came out with a bucket of water to keep down the dust on a hot summer's day.

THE HIGH STREET MARKET

The railway changed the balance between Marsh Street and Wood Street. The former was re-named High Street in 1882, in response to a petition from sixty local traders and at the end of a period which had seen rapid growth of shops on Marsh Street and Hoe Street compared to Wood Street and Orford Road. The dominance of the High Street was confirmed with the coming of the costermongers, with the first stalls recorded in 1885. What has developed into the longest street market in London was not regulated until 1890, but then fights between the costers over who was to have the best site led to regulations being drawn up in 1890. No stall could be put up before 8am and the rivals had to wait in side streets with their barrows for the rush for the best pitch.

The early stalls were simple barrows, but these later evolved into flat topped hand carts, with rods to support a canvas cover. The wheels were brightly painted and sometimes carved, while there would also be a large sign board to go above the stall. The markets also stayed open later and as dark evenings drew in, lights were needed to allow the customers to see, and prevent theft. Initially the costers used naphtha flares and one resident remembered the scene before the First World War:

> Naphtha lighting shed a fitful stinking spluttering glow until at least midnight on Saturdays. You could, within a few yards, buy a pet, have a tooth pulled, fill your market bag with shopping for sixpence, adorn yourself with a 'genuine' Indian scent, safeguard yourself with a bottle of a 'wonder cure all", be weighed, be measured and be robbed.

But all this activity came with shouts from the traders, the patter of the quick talking medicine salesmen and the cries of delight or outrage from shoppers. And the smell.

> The smell came from the rubbish piled ankle deep in the gutters, spoiled eggs, discarded fish, smelling salts, cheese, second hand clothing, third hand shoes, saveloys, faggots, hot potatoes, hokey pokey ice cream, cough candies, hot fritters and jars of pickled fish.

There were many who tried their hand at trading. An Italian photographer called Matioli clothed his sons in the tawdry uniforms of obscure countries. A medicine man dressed himself up as an American marshal from the Wild West and sold rhubarb plant health cures. One, George

123. All change on the High Street. The demolition of the Ivy House and Gillards in 1932 to make way for the parade of shops (nos 219-239) built on the site. The tower of Walthamstow Palace theatre rises in the distance. Watercolour by T. Stuart Milner, 1932.

124. Peak's store in the High Street in the 1920s.

125. St James Street c.1905.

126. Mr and Mrs Philpot, with Mr Philpot's sailor brother outside their shop at 84 Somerset Road about 1912.

127. Sainsbury's in the High Street, c.1914.

Borwick, who had invented a powder to help with baking, first sold his product on the High Street. But not all were so successful. In the 1880s, Alf Ball ran a boxing booth where shoppers could take on a professional fighter for a prize if they could stay the course. When this palled the booth was given over to a sad old lion with gloves on its front paws, who was assaulted by a boxer to make it snarl. It was a blessing when the audience did not rise to the cruelty and the booths closed. In 1891 the Salvation Army bought the site and built a citadel on it.

But an empty shop could be had cheaply and a number were taken for freak shows in the 1890s. There was the Electric Lady whose hand rested in a glass of water, which gave a mild electric shock to anyone doing the same. There was a 'Lion Faced Woman' and there was a mermaid – a girl seated behind a large glass tank with a very crude tail concealing the chair she was sitting on.

In 1932 the Borough Council introduced a licensing system for the costers, using the money to help pay for clearing up the aftermath of the markets, and at the same time ending disputes over the best sites.

Small family shops on the High Street were also joined by multiples from the turn of the century, including Woolworth's, Lipton's and Sainsbury's, whose double fronted shop and boxes of produce on the pavement, was at 18 High Street in 1910. Marks and Spencer's took over a London Penny Bazaar shop at 19 High Street in 1914, and traded from there until 1931. Wood Street retained smaller concerns, including Carlo Gatti, an Italian firm which delivered ice blocks to local businesses in the 1930s, before the days of refrigeration. Today the street is best known for the antiques trade, which developed in the early 1970s. The Georgian Village, the precursor of the traders, was established a little before 1973.

128. Shops in Hoe Street, c.1920.

129. The Albion Bakery in Beulah Road.

initially approved but then hastily rescinded a few days later, while a boxing promoter wanting to use the hall was rebuffed. The club is now based on Hoe Street, and is among the oldest working men's clubs in the country.

Other self-help groups included Freemasons – the first local lodge was formed in 1877, whose membership grew out of informal gatherings at the Chequers and whose minimum subscription level of five guineas made it exclusively middle class. Friendly Societies provided members with coffee socials, fruit and ice cream banquets, and later the formation of a United Council of Walthamstow Friendly Societies in 1889 enabled the organisation of outings for members to resorts like Clacton. Some allowed women to join, but many met on licensed premises and were effectively limited to men only. A meeting to establish a local Co-operative Society was held in the Workmen's Hall in 1889, with the formative influences being W.G. Cluff, local developer and politician, and E. Good, a builder. The resultant society was able to provide food at lower prices, and make donations to local charities. An education committee organised a programme of monthly lectures, but the membership did not rise to expected levels and in 1899 the society merged with the Stratford Co-operative.

Some self-help was supported by local charities. In 1834 Lord Maynard made a grant of copyhold land alongside Haggar Lane to the newly created Spade Husbandry Charity, with the intention that the eleven acres be utilised for allotments and the rents used to reduce the poor rate. The land was diminished by the sale of 3.5 acres in 1939, but survived into the 1970s. Allotments were also created on the former common land at Higham Hill and Markhouse Common in 1851. As with many current allotment societies, there was a waiting list in the 1890s, when gaining a place depended on the length of residence in Walthamstow.

The Leyton, Walthamstow, Woodford and Wanstead Horticultural Society organised spring and summer shows from the 1850s, and by the 1870s these were open to non-members There was a Lea Bridge Amateur Horticultural Society with annual shows from 1855 to 1871 and in the 1880s the Walthamstow Floricultural and Markhouse Common Allotments and Garden Protection Society offered a place for working class gardeners.

CHURCH SOCIALS

Local churches and chapels all maintained a range of local activities – choirs, temperance groups, bands of hope. St Mary's Church provided very little in the 1870s, but by 1885 there were no less than twelve societies, which included a fife and drum band, a savings club, a shoe club, sewing and knitting classes, a maternity society, a floricultural society and a cricket club. There were also regular Sunday school treats. The church had recognised the special needs of poorer people –for example special services were arranged for the navvies working on the construction of the Chingford branch in 1866 and 1869. But the established order and the allocated pew system mitigated against sustained efforts to attract churchgoers from the poorer incomers.

By contrast the Lighthouse Methodist Church was founded as a missionary activity from members of Hackney's Pembury Grove circuit. The first open air meeting was held in 1887 and by 1893 the Lighthouse church, with space for a congregation of 850 had been built. There were 23 societies by 1904, including loan clubs and even a Christmas Goose Club. The first ministers were prepared to discuss controversial issues and people could come in working clothes. The hall was also used for ballad concerts, lantern shows, limelight lectures and Pleasant Sunday Afternoon concerts, in which the audiences' experience would be celebrated in comic songs like *Boarding House Bores.* In 1894 a handbill proclaimed "Say what is this place ? Why it's the People's Cathedral for the crowds of Walthamstow".

STREET AND HALL

But for many working class men, the main attractions would have remained the High Street stalls and activities available in Epping Forest or on the marshes – the latter offering rabbit coursing, whippet racing and bare knuckle fighting. Travelling performers used what venues they could – on Easter Monday 1871 Mr Talliot's First Class Company set up opposite the Coach and Horses on Marsh Street. Wombwell's travelling menagerie and Sanger's Circus were also regular visitors in the 1890s In the 1950s people still remembered the street parades of elephants, camels, painted ladies on gilded carts, and tumbling clowns, and Sanger's Circus drew an audience of 11,000 to its 'monster hippodrome at Walthamstow in 1891.

132. The public hall in Orford Road. From the Houghton album c.1870.

The hall at the Lighthouse had met a need for performance space. In March 1856 the actress Fanny Kemble was billed to give two readings from Shakespeare's *Julius Caesar* and *A Midsummer Night's Dream* on 7 and 21 April, but the best space available was the hall of the Infant School. So the promoters of the Public Hall on Orford Road hoped to meet a need – and make money. The hall opened in 1865 and established a regular programme which included music hall turns. It was used by local groups like the Walthamstow Hand Bell Ringers and the Walthamstow Minstrels who formed part of the 1874 season. They combined for 'The Horrible Walthamstow Ghost' plus "a side splitting Darkey sketch, 'the Medical Institute, with Negro walk and Breakdown'". Black and white minstrel acts were not enough to sustain the hall, and the company went into liquidation in 1876. The premises were incorporated into the town hall of 1877 and were still available for social use. In May 1878 John Hitchman, the head lessee of the Fitzwygram estate, made use of it for a bit of community building. He invited the tenants and owners of the various houses on the estate, by then virtually complete, to a social evening to get to know each other, and in the hope of seeing the formation of a 'collective association'. The hall survived along with the town hall to form part of the later Connaught Hospital, but sadly it was demolished when the hospital site was redeveloped in the 1980s.

THEATRE AND CINEMA

We have already encountered John Read as one of the backers of the Working Men's Club. He had a strong interest in music and founded the Walthamstow Musical Society in 1867. In 1857 he entered into a partnership with a local builder, John Cropley (also a local board member), to build the Victoria Hall on Hoe Street. Read wanted a place to stage concerts of his own and other composers' works. At least one contemporary journalist was impressed:

> As a ballroom, it will be unsurpassed, while the glass roofed annexe, 35 feet long by 10 feet wide, will give that desirable adjunct, a conservatory, where, amid the gentle quivering leaves and sheltering shrubs, soft sentiments and tender vows will often find expression after the stimulating effect of the mazy dance.

133. Walthamstow Palace in the High Street, 1905.

The hall was a success but was sold in 1896 to James Warwick Buckland, who converted it into a theatre and staged melodramas, like *On the Frontier*, set in the American Wild West. He leased it to Rollo Balmain and it became the King's Theatre in 1901. A show called *Purgatory*, featuring a monk and his lover, caused trouble when it transferred to Collin's Music Hall in Islington as the manager there felt that it was not a family show and took it off after one night. Legal action between the two managements ensued, with Balmain emerging victorious. However, the judge felt that the work was not one that should be performed in a music hall that had no theatrical licence, since it ought to have been subject to the control of the Lord Chamberlain. In the event melodrama and risqué drama were not enough to compete against the new attraction of the cinema and the theatre closed in 1907 and, reverting to its old name, Victoria Hall, became a cinema. It was demolished in 1930 for the construction of the Granada Cinema, seating 3000 people.

The Walthamstow Palace theatre of varieties, with its twin towers, opened on the High Street on 28 December 1903. The first act was Fred Karno's comedy troupe, which was later to include future stars like Stan Laurel and Charlie Chaplin. Other acts of the day included Harry Lauder and Marie Lloyd. There were seven to ten acts per night and a new show every Saturday. Later short dramas from well-known stories became popular, and both *East Lynne* and *David Copperfield* were so treated in 1906. The Palace staged regular variety shows plus the obligatory Christmas season pantomime and an annual circus visit in the 1920s and 1930s, but after the Second World War it was difficult to bring in audiences, despite semi-nude shows. The Countess de Ia Marr took over the theatre in 1952 to revive real drama, but the appetite for local theatre had gone in the 1950s and the venture failed. The Palace closed on 24 February 1964 and after a period of dereliction was demolished in 1960. Palace Parade was built on the site.

It was at the Victoria Hall that a Walthamstow audience got its first chance to see moving film when Edward Turner put on a show on 10 June 1896, charging two guineas. Turner also made his

134. The twin towers of the Walthamstow Palace.

own films and supplied short topical pieces to penny gaffs and local houses. Another local establishment, the Prince's Pavilion, on the High Street started showing films in 1909. It was rebuilt in 1912 to become Walthamstow's first purpose-built cinema, seating 1000 people, but in rather Spartan surroundings of wooden benches and bare roof girders. A rival, the Carlton, opened in November 1913. The architect was J. Williams Dunsford, who had also designed the Central Library, and customers were greeted by a richly carpeted entrance with oak-panelled walls and hanging antique styled lanterns. A magnificent pipe organ was added in 1925, to provide music for the silent films, replacing the six-strong Carlton Orchestra which had previously performed.

There were nine local cinemas by 1914, of which six remained by 1951 and only two by 1965. One of these was the Regal, which had started life as the Highams Park Electric Theatre in 1912 at the junction of Hale End and Beech Hall roads. Renamed the Regal in 1928, it was first in the field locally with the new talking pictures and was rebuilt in 1935. It became a bingo hall in 1963, but still showed the occasional film until 1970. Another closed cinema was the Empire on the Bell corner of Hoe Street. This had been built by Good Brothers in 1913, and after it closed in the late 1960s had a period as a sex club. In 2001 it survived as a pool hall.

Prince's Pavilion was demolished in 1930 and replaced by the Dominion cinema, which held 1685 people and whose fittings included a real Wurlitzer organ, imported from the USA. After the demise of the silent film, the organ continued to be used for recitals but it was sold off in 1958 and the cinema became a bingo hall in 1961. The Carlton closed in 1964. The premises were incorporated into a supermarket, which was demolished in advance of the construction of the Selborne Walk shopping centre in the mid 1980s. The Granada was badly damaged by a flying bomb in 1944, but later restored. It was converted to two small cinemas in 1973 and now as EMD Cinema, is Walthamstow's sole surviving public film venue.

NEWSPAPERS

One source for what any area can offer is the local newspaper. Walthamstow has some early connections with the press - Robert MacFarlane (1734-1804), who ran a private school at Shern Lodge, had been editor of the *Morning Chronicle* and *The London Packet.* Edward Lloyd, whose first newspaper, *the Penny Sunday Times and People's Police Gazette,* appeared in 1840 and who later became famous for *Lloyds Weekly News,* bought Water House in 1857, giving his name to the present Lloyd Park. But local affairs were reported in the Essex county newspapers, which were less and less concerned with the affairs of the parts of the county on the borders of London. Walthamstow's first local paper did not appear until 1870, when printer Joseph Shillinglaw based at Chestnut Walk, Lea Bridge Road, produced the *Walthamstow Chronicle and Leyton Intelligence.* The paper opened an office on Grosvenor Park Road and Shillinglaw was helped by a Mr Cruickshank, a comedian who had performed at the Surrey Theatre. Shillinglaw also produced local directories and had published Ebenezer Clarke's history in 1861, but the newspaper was not a success and was bought out by its rival, the *Walthamstow Guardian.*

The first issue of the local *Guardian* – originally the *Walthamstow and Leyton Guardian* appeared on 6 May 1876, and was a four-sheet affair published by F. Smith, a bookseller and stationer in Orford Road. It was backed by three local businessmen, and was supposedly politically neutral, but one of the three, Samuel Herbert, went on to become controlling editor. Herbert was a Tory who allowed his views to colour the paper and had a tendency to suppress news he disliked. When the paper became a limited company in 1890 he moved to be Managing Director and Chairman, and it was only six months before his death in 1919 that control passed to those of other views. William Mallinson and A.M. Mathews then took over. Mathews aspired to be a Liberal MP and while he achieved his ambition, the *Guardian* became markedly less right wing.

The new management moved the offices to no. 559 Lea Bridge Road and in 1923 also moved the printing to Walthamstow – previously all issues had been printed in the City of London. The paper moved to Guardian House on Forest Road in 1935.

There was a range of mostly short-lived papers that tilted against the *Guardian.* One, the irreverent *Walthamstow Whip* nicknamed its older rival 'Granny'. It took a Progressive view, but lasted only a year from 1897-98. The *Walthamstow Express* began as a local edition of the *Stratford Express* in 1882, but after a few local editions reverted to the Stratford title, with local Walthamstow sections. The *Walthamstow and District Times,* a paper supporting the Liberals, founded in 1901 was in trouble by 1903, with all the founding capital used up. E.R. Alexander, the printers, took it on in lieu of the money they were owed and sold it on to a local builder, S.W. Robinson in 1912. Robinson, who was later to be an Essex county councillor and the Liberal MP for Chelmsford quickly regretted his purchase after finding out the state of the finances and the circulation and had to be taken to court to be compelled to complete the purchase. The paper ceased publication in August 1914.

But the most sensational scourge of the *Guardian* was the *Walthamstow Reporter.* The first issue appeared on 26 October 1894, devoted to "active progressive Radicalism and Labour interests." It was edited by Walthamstow's own local firebrand, J.J. McSheedy, whom we have encountered already in the troubled politics of the period. McSheedy was never afraid to put his views forward in the clearest fashion. This is from his first editorial:

> As a journalist for many years, one does not hesitate to assert that the two existing local purveyors of hogwash would disgrace the lowest dregs of modern journalism. They have bartered every vestige of even common journalistic decency for their miserable transitory message of pottage. You cannot rely upon a single statement of fact, their hideous misrepresentation of the democrats of the town [who could McSheedy have had in mind?], their shameless suppression of the truth, their *suggestio falsi* and *suppresso veri,* their slavish adulation and support of their patrons and paymasters under every circumstance, their unblushing ignorance and their unhesitating support of all that is locally mean, contemptible, unreal and unjust, have become a by-word and a grievous public scandal and disgrace.

It was no wonder that it took less than twelve months for *The Reporter* to face its first libel writ. The *Guardian* estimated its rival's circulation reached 2000 in 1895 and the following year the paper was enlarged in size and printed on pink paper to make its allegiance absolutely clear. But it led a troubled life. The first manager and publisher embezzled money in his trust, the second withdrew after McSheedy had denounced his writings in the paper and as libel actions mounted up, the shareholders diminished. In 1903 there was a showdown between them and McSheedy quit abruptly, but not before he had come to an arrangement with the printers, who refused to print any further issues. All other printers were engaged in printing election material, and so that, for the *Reporter,* was that. However McSheedy and the printers were able to move into the immediate production of a successor, *The Walthamstow Recorder,* which appeared on the same day that the *Reporter* issued the announcement of its demise in the form of a handbill.

McSheedy's second venture was not to last long. In 1902 he had been successfully sued for libel by C.T. Wilkinson, a solicitor and a councillor of the Moderate Party (effectively the local Conservatives). Wilkinson had won earlier actions against McSheedy, one of which prevented him being named by the *Reporter* – a black spot was used instead. McSheedy had been bankrupted by the judgement and Wilkinson had become a trustee under the terms of the bankruptcy. In 1905 Wilkinson instituted an action to recover £30 from Walthamstow Council for adverts it had placed in the *Walthamstow Recorder.* £5 14s of this was claimed by Mrs McSheedy, and when only £10 5s was obtained from the Council, Mrs McSheedy received the full sum she had claimed in her capacity as the owner of the *Recorder,* her husband having made the transfer on 1 April 1905. Wilkinson appealed and the court decided that McSheedy was not entitled to transfer his property as a bankrupt and by these devious actions, Wilkinson obtained his true end, which was the closure of *The Recorder.*

In the aftermath of the debacle of the *Reporter,* those radicals alienated by McSheedy's wilder linguistic and political flings attempted a resurrection. The *Walthamstow Gazette* had appeared as a free advertising paper in July 1903. On 1 January 1904 it was merged with the *Reporter* to form *The Walthamstow Reporter and Gazette,* running to eight pages. It assured its readers – and shareholders – in its first number that "one essential feature in the policy which will be adopted will be the entire elimination of all personalities from its criticisms." Maybe so, but the bland unexciting coverage did not sell copies, and the paper returned to be a free advertising sheet four months later and it died, politely and quietly in 1908.

Just as fugitive were the papers produced by political parties. The Walthamstow branch of the Social-Democratic Foundation produced the *Socialist Critic* in March 1900, which lasted barely a year, while only three issues survive of the *Walthamstow Municipal Gazette,* produced in 1921 by the local Labour Party.

Local papers varied in size and frequency - most were weekly, and while some ran to sixteen pages, other were smaller. All mixed national and local news, and from the 1890s added features and general articles. Many of the proprietors had started as printers or continued to fund papers from their printing businesses. Others remained as printers, but in one celebrated case, a firm got ensnared in a major legal dispute.

Charles and Benjamin Buck had founded Buck Brothers in the 1890s, working from various addresses in Leyton, Bishopsgate, Old Kent Road, Mare Street and Hackney Road before opening the Marx Press in Stainforth Road in Walthamstow in 1905. They printed the *Walthamstow Reporter and Gazette,* but in 1912 Guy Bowman asked them to print his newspaper, *The Syndicalist.* There was unrest in the mines and a national strike seemed likely, which could lead to the use of the military so Bowman wrote and published an article urging soldiers not to shoot striking miners. The government promptly instigated a prosecution of Bowman and the Buck brothers under the Incitement to Mutiny Act of 1797. George Lansbury, Will Thorne and Josiah Wedgwood stood surety for the prisoners, but they were convicted on 22 March. Bowman was sentenced to nine months with hard labour and the Buck brothers to six months. The ensuing outcry resulted in the formation of a Free Speech Defence Committee. On appeal the sentences were reduced to two months for Bowman and one month for the Bucks. After their release W.R. Harding helped them restore the business and remained a partner until he sold out while on war service in 1915. Buck Brothers continued to print local newspapers until they sold their business to the Walthamstow Press in 1937.

135. Loading hay at Moons Farm, 1912.

Working world

FARMING

Until the mid nineteenth century agriculture was the principal source of employment in Walthamstow, though from the sixteenth century grassland predominated. Local landlords could impose rises in rents for conversion of pasture to arable. The period of war against France from the late 1790s saw an increase in arable acreage, rising from 425 acres in 1794 to 829 acres in 1801, in which year the main crops were wheat and oats, with smaller crops of peas, barley, potatoes, rye, beans and turnips or rape.

There were also speciality crops. Hops were grown at Moons Farm in the sixteenth century and there were hopfields near Boundary Road in the late nineteenth century. Samuel Pepys recalled the vines in William Batten's garden in the 1660s, and thought Batten's wine the equal of foreign imports.

By 1843 there were 2628 acres of pasture or meadow and 915 of arable. The largest farmers were Robert Wragg, the stage coach master, whose 312 acres included Clay Street and the Elms farms. The Salisbury Hall home farm was 224 acres, and Low Hall, farmed by Charles Burrell, a cattle-dealer, was 228 acres. Burrell, who was supplying the Smithfield market, added a bullock house, cattle lairs, pounds for sorting sheep and stock and his own slaughterhouse. There were about a dozen other farms at the same date, ranging in size from 45 acres to go 130 acres.

Not all the farmers had long-standing roots in the area. The Smith family were pin makers in Great Dover Street in the mid nineteenth century, and initially took a lease on Inks Green farm at Chingford. They moved on quickly as the son of the previous owner had been convicted for murder and came to Moons Farm on Billet Road in 1868. They farmed ten acres round Moons, a further four acres of glebe land in Billet Lane and 14.5 acres by the Ching on the site of Walthamstow dog stadium. With its moat and pond, Moons Farm made an ideal playground for the children, who took tea up to their father and his men when they were out on the fields by the Ching during harvest. In the pause between the harvest Mr Smith senior made his son waterwheels, squeakers and other toys from the willow branches over the stream. When not needed to help, the children could fish the Ching, and Mr Smith junior remembered netting the pools at the time of Queen

136. *The barn at Moon's Farm, shortly before it was dismantled. Photograph 1926.*

137. *Loading hay at Bull's farm in 1911.*

Victoria's Golden Jubilee in 1887 and catching dace, pike and roach.

Small and large farmers were able to draw on cottagers for their labour. In the farm cottages of Chapel End lived the Tarlings and the Izzards, who worked to bring in the potatoes, and pick twitch and stones from the fields. Hirings were in the Billet public house, open all day except Sunday, and farm agreements were also settled here. Prior to the licensing laws introduced in the First World War any one travelling more than three miles could get a drink out of opening hours – and at the Billet no-one asked too many questions as to where a man actually lived ...

Chapel End also supported related tradesmen – Charles Kite at Kite's Corner made harnesses for the horse teams, slaughtered unwanted horses and were brake proprietors. Next door the Davis family were carpenters and gardeners. Some farms went on to specialise – among the farmers at Salisbury Hall were the Halfhead brothers, who bred pigs. In its last years St John's Farm on the corner of Billett Lane was a pig factory, and the stench of boiling bones had to be endured by the locals.

Some help for smaller farmers came from their neighbours. The Smiths were helped by John Hitchman of Wadham Farm, who had come to the area in 1867, and was able to borrow farm tools and even men to help with the harvesting. Hitchman was a temperance man, so his workers got a non-alcoholic oatmeal drink at harvest rather than the customary beer. On some farms the horses had to know their own way back in the evening, carrying a carter swaying and sleeping off a skinful in the back of the cart.

There was only one dairyman listed in local directories, but by 1906 there were 46, three of whom kept their own cows. One was Hitchman, who also leased the Clay Street farm and began direct sales of milk in the 1880s. In 1918 the business of John Hitchman and Sons was bought out by D.A. Davies, a partner in another Walthamstow firm, Davies and Williams. The new company traded as Hitchman Dairies and operated from a purpose-built milk processing plant on Walthamstow Avenue from 1938. Hitchman's later became part of the Unigate group. In 2001 the company name was still visible on their former factory building from the North Circular Road.

A number of Scots farmers came to Essex in the 1890s and one, James Fergueson, came to Walthamstow with a train load of farming implements. He impressed his neighbours with his hard work, and they were intrigued by his different techniques of hay making, training one man to lead two carts – and the polished bottoms of his milk churns! Fergueson also brought down Ayrshire cows, made his own cheese, and staffed his dairy with Scots dairymaids – of whom nothing more is recorded, so perhaps they did not stay for any length of time.

The development of Walthamstow gradually reduced farmland. Low Hall was bought by the local board in 1875-7, but initially only part was used as a sewage plant, though by 1907 only 36 acres remained. The last of Salisbury Hall's farmland was sold in 1904. The last of the large farms to be sold for building were the Chestnuts (formerly Clay Street farm) whose 67 acres were sold to Walthamstow UDC in 1919, and Wadham Lodge, which had been farmed from 1898 by John Hitchman, was sold for housing and a sports ground in 1919. Moons Farm, the Smith's old home, was sold in 1927. Monoux Grove now occupies the site of the farmhouse. Moons Barn was dismantled and intended for preservation, but storage problems led to the destruction of the timbers. Bulls Farm on the north side of Billet Road was the very last of Walthamstow's working farms when it was sold in 1950. McEntee Avenue, Romany Gardens and adjoining roads cover the site.

The proximity of the London market encouraged market gardening and plant nurseries and three nurserymen were in business in the parish in 1839. One of these was James Pamplin, originally based at Whipps Cross, but also with land in Leyton, and from 1860 using the former nursery of James Gollop on the east side of Wood Street, where his successes included orange trees. Although the Smith family saw the coming of the railway as the end of a rural haven and had to cope with a lot more pilfering of fruit and theft of chickens, the railway would also have offered improved transport for the market gardeners. In 1863 there were thirteen gardeners and five nurserymen and florists - perhaps using the station at Lea Bridge - but the pace of building gradually swept over the nursery grounds. Pamplin's business shut in 1893 and by 1906 there were only one market gardener and two nurserymen left.

MILLS

The Domesday survey of the parish mentions a mill which existed in 1066 and twenty years later. This would have been water powered from the artificially created mill stream and there are successive medieval references to this mill. In 1611 there were said to be four mills. In the years before the English Civil War the Walthamstow mill is likely to have been one of those on the Lea used for making gunpowder, since the adjoining land was known as Powder Mill marsh in 1699. But by 1653 the mill was making paper, and Charles Maynard sold it out of the manor in 1659 to John Samyne of Bow. The mill stream became the Paper Mill River up to go 1703, after which the mill was used in leather dressing, successively by Pierre Montier (1703), Peter Lefevre from 1711 and Daniel Lefevre from 1713 to 1723. From the early 1740s the mill produced linseed oil, until 1806 when the recently rebuilt mills were sold.

The purchasers were the British Copper Company, which from 1808 rolled copper and struck tokens, intended to meet the lack of copper coins in general circulation and issued by a number of companies of the period. Successive owners continued rolling copper until 1857, when the majority of the plant was sold for use in the Swansea area. A crane, used to load the ingots on to barges, survives by the wharf. In 1860 the East London Waterworks Company bought the mill for use as a pumping station. It survives today, latterly used as a store by Thames Water. The British Coppermill Company built ten houses for their employees downstream from the mill, later demolished after the takeover by the ELWC. The mill house was demolished in 1941.

Walthamstow's windmill had been built by John Hawkes a millwright from Whitechapel, at Tile Kiln Hill in 1676, on the site of the modern Oakhill Gardens. Hawkes also built the miller's house, and a late eighteenth-century illustration shows that the mill, by then in poor condition, was by that stage a post mill with a brick round house surrounding the circular base. From 1690 to 1759 the Haines family had the mill – and when business was slow also sold their own beer. They were presented at the manor court for so doing in 1745, 1746 and 1747 – the successive complaints showed that it was not easy to stop them,

138. The Copper Mill showing the old crane and wharf.

and in fact they eventually obtained a licence from the Epping Forest court in 1750. The mill survived in a derelict condition until 1800, when it blew down in a storm. It appears on the preliminary drawings of the 1805 Ordnance Survey map, but was deleted from the printed version – presumably someone had established that the mill had definitely ceased to be. The Mill Cottage survived as a private house - a later occupant was Edward Forster junior, the botanist and philanthropist, who took it from 1826-1838. The house went in 1890 and the site is now covered by Oakhill Gardens.

BRICKS, TILES AND POTS

Manorial land near the forest was also used to make bricks and tiles in the seventeenth century. A site at Higham Bushes was used by John Russell to build a tile and brick-kiln in 1607 and his son George built a house, stipulated as having at least six rooms under the terms of his lease, shortly after 1655. Tile making had ceased by 1796 and Tile Kiln House was demolished in 1820. An adjoining business, which started around 1768, was bought out in 1787, probably to ensure that Highams has no industry based next to its grounds. The overgrown pits from the diggings survived near the Bridle Path in the 1970s. Later brickfields were established to support nineteenth-century local builders, mostly in the area of Chapel End and Folly Lane.

The Pettit family was operating 'London Potteries' in Haringey in the 1860s when they spotted a potential site for a new works at Higham Hill while delivering tiles in the area. There was an outcrop of blue London Clay in the area, and George and Ernest Pettit and their father established the works on the bend in Folly Lane. The family occupied a set of cottages built with secondhand brick at the top of the lane, whose amenities consisted of water from an iron pump and a weekly mail collection, announced by a blast on the postie's whistle. On ground owned by the Walthamstow Parochial Charities, the family produced unglazed pots from clay ground in a barrel powered by a blindfolded horse walking in a circle. With the growth of market gardening in the Lea Valley, the business switched to making plant pots. Steam power replaced the horse, but coal shortages forced closure about 1944.

139. Pettit & Son's pottery in Folly Lane, Higham Hill, c.1890s.

OTHER EMPLOYERS

Other than the mills, there was relatively little manufacturing activity in the parish before the nineteenth century. A number of moneyers – contractors who minted coins for the royal mint – were based in Walthamstow from the late sixteenth century and in 1663 were exempted from the hearth tax. Four generations of the Collard family, whose links with Walthamstow went back to the fifteenth century, were master moneyers from 1684 to 1791.

Samuel Tull set up a workshop to spin pack thread intending to use the labour of vagrants and workhouse paupers, but the vestry withdrew its support in 1772. More jobs were provided by the gentry, and nearly 11% of the parish was in domestic service in 1831. Some would have lived in-house and a few would have notched up many years of service to one family. Others would have performed a range of tasks for a number of families, like Benjamin Warwick (*ill. 67*), gardener to the Houghton family in the 1870s. Others produced or sold specialist goods like lace, perfumes, umbrellas, china and toys and the Victorian passion for the piano employed piano tuners and music teachers.

The growth of Walthamstow supported a range of local builders - there were five listed in local directories in 1866 and 37 by 1890. After the Chingford branch railway opened a number of small works were established, making items like picture frames, mechanical toys, surgical instruments, fancy boxes and ginger beer, and some were to grow in the 1890s, when Walthamstow attracted businesses looking for space to build larger works, or to establish themselves in an area where the growing population might consider local employment rather than working in central London.

NEW INDUSTRIES

Among these were 'new' industries – electrical engineering, motor vehicles, scientific instruments, and plastics. Alongside these were craft trades, including tinware, billiard tables, pianos and baby carriages. There were 23 makers of bicycles and bicycle parts listed in 1910, a substantial part of the total capacity in Essex at the time. Clothing firms, many employing outworkers, produced collars, shirts and neckwear. Businesses took advantage of available land in the north of the parish, at Hale End, Blackhorse Lane and along Forest Road, as well as on Hoe Street and Shernhall Street.

The outcome was a very diverse range of industries, many of which survived into the 1970s. Among the food and drink makers were A.H. Simpkins, established in 1887 who made mineral water and were based on Hoe Street for many years until closure in 1939. Gillard & Co's pickles have already been noted as an uncomfortably close neighbour to Monoux Grammar school on the High Street, where they were founded in the Chestnuts in 1892, which they later renamed Vintry Works. The firm later moved to Westbury Road in 1937. Ice cream makers included Shales who relocated from Southend in 1934 and ceased trading in 1959 and an Italian company which operated in Church Lane up to the mid 1980s.

A fifty-year connection with flavourings and fragrances began in 1956 when A. Boake Roberts of West Ham set up a factory on Blackhorse Lane. The company became part of the Bush Boake Allen group in 1966, incorporating firms with links to Islington and Hackney. The factory, now part of International Flavourings and Fragrances, had wound down much of its manufacturing activities by 2001, with the site planned for closure at the time of writing.

ENGINEERING AND ELECTRICAL FACTORIES

Engineering and electrical goods making formed a significant part of Walthamstow's businesses in the twentieth century. Factories on Blackhorse Lane included W.B. Bawn and Co, who made tractors and road wagon tanks and moved there in 1940 after their factory at Poplar was destroyed in the blitz. For thirty years their works entrance was straddled by a life-sized figure of a seventeenth-century helmsman, which had come from Poplar and went with them in 1970 when they moved to Suffolk. Baird and Tatlock, originally a Glasgow firm, which made scientific instruments, bought Higham Lodge in 1902 and employed 600 people in 1970. An apprentices' project, a magnificent model bench, complete with miniature gas taps, made in the company's works, is on display at Vestry House Museum. Photographic equipment was made by Spratt Brothers originally of Hackney, at their newly established Ensign Works in Fulborne Road from 1908. After mergers with other concerns, the company became Barnet Ensign Ross Ltd in 1948. It left Walthamstow in 1954.

The Fuller-Wenstrom Electrical Manufacturing Company moved to Blackhorse Lane in 1905

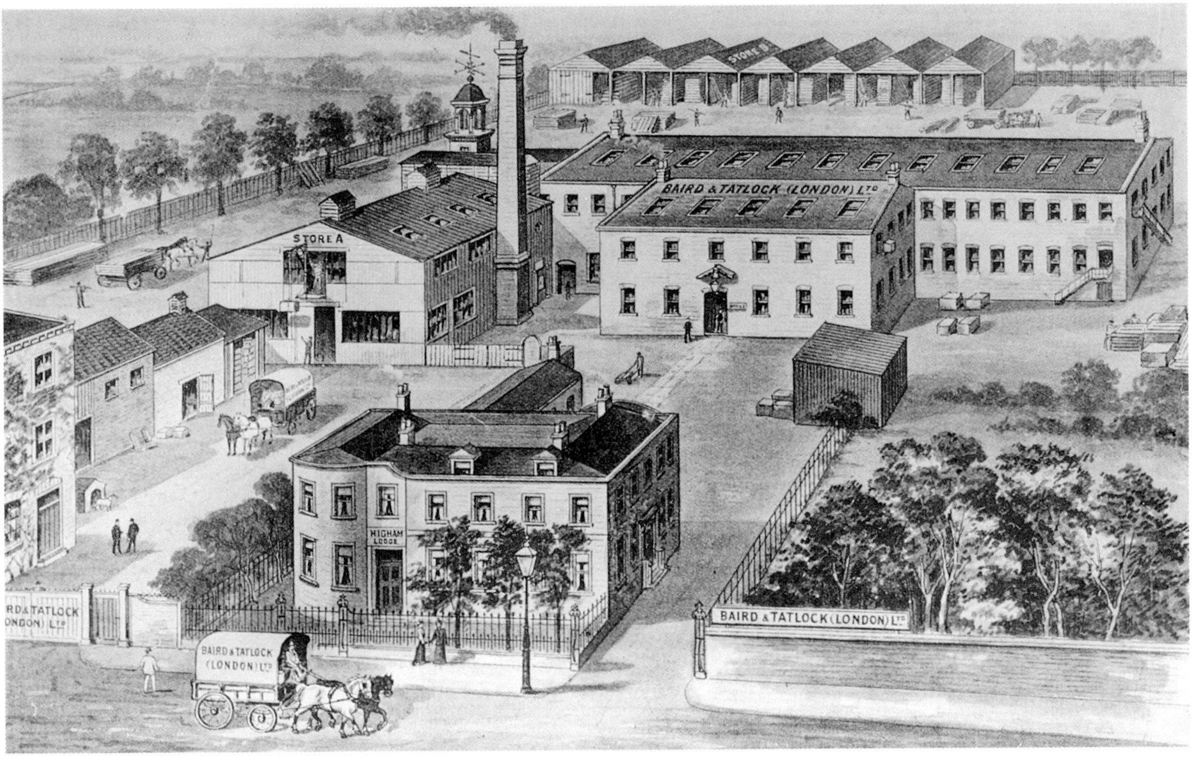

140. The Baird and Tatlock factory, including the graceful Higham Lodge.

where they assembled and distributed motors imported from Sweden. Ten years later they moved to Fulbourne Road and expanded by acquiring the empty Ensign works there in 1955. The Swedish link continued, but the company also made transformers and as Fuller Electric was acquired by the Brush Group in 1957. Another concern to move to Blackhorse Lane, was the Mica Insulator Company, in 1902. The company expanded its works five years later and in 1928-9 when it became a major employer of women. The total workforce rose from 600 during the First World War to 1,700 in 1955. It later became part of the GEC group of companies. Household names in electrical and related goods included Phillips Records, who set up a pressing plant at Walthamstow Avenue in 1958 and Ever Ready, who built a large battery making factory on Forest Road in 1931-2.

DRIVING AND FLYING

Walthamstow has a special place in the history of motor vehicles. Frederick Bremer established a motor cycle works at Grosvenor Park Road around 1912, trading until around 1926. But ten years earlier Bremer had produced Britain's very first car with an internal combustion engine, which he drove down the Woodford Road in 1894, preceded, as the law of the time demanded, by a red flag. Bremer never put his design into production, but the original car survived and was given to Vestry House Museum in 1933. It was put back into working order in 1962-3 and completed a run to Brighton in the veteran car race in 1965. Today the car is back on display in the former workhouse yard in the Museum.

Vanguard Motor Omnibus Company made buses on Blackhorse Lane in 1906, and was taken over by the London General Omnibus Company in 1908, which in turn formed AEC in 1911, continuing to make buses in Walthamstow until 1927. The Ford Motor Company also had an engineering plant in Blackhorse Lane for twenty years from 1947.

It was to motor cars that Alliot Verdon Roe first turned when he resigned as a marine engineer in 1902, but it was the novel area of aircraft design that lured him away. After an unsuccessful period in the USA he returned to England in 1907, winning a second prize in a *Daily Mail* compe-

141. Bremer and friend Mr Bates with the car after a journey to Crystal Palace.

tition in that year for the best flying machine models. Roe began to experiment with triplane design, but needed a large open space to test his prototype. Early in 1909 he got permission to use Walthamstow Marsh and rented a couple of railway arches to use as storage. He boarded up the ends, but had to put up with leaks from the brick arch and occasional floods. There were no windows, so letting in the light also meant letting in the weather. There were spectators - with helpful comments like 'What time are you going up governor ?'. But there was little sense that this was something momentous - not surprising considering what usually followed:

> We then endeavoured to start up the engine, a task which usually took at least a quarter of an hour. When it was started and warmed, I would then give the signal, 'let's go', and the machine then tore over the ground followed by my helpers carrying tools, pieces of timber and other necessary appliances to cope with the repairs necessary after the almost inevitable crash.

And there were days when the marshes were wanted for grazing or playing football. But perseverance had its reward. The nine horsepower motorcycle engine managed to get the plane airborne for distances of up to 100 feet, and on 23 July 1909 the aircraft, dubbed the 'yellow terror' from the oiled paper stretched over the fuselage, travelled over 900 feet at the grand height of ten feet off the ground. Roe had become the first person to fly over any part of Britain in a British built and powered aircraft. Roe left his marshes retreat at the end of 1909, and with help from his brother, set up the AVRO Company in the following year. From such uncertain beginnings came such famous planes as the Lancaster bomber and the Shackletons that had so many years of reconnaissance work through the twentieth century. Roe's achievement was marked by a Blue Plaque on the railway arches in the early 1980s.

FURNITURE AND TOYS

Furniture making moved into the Lea Valley from inner city locations like Hackney and Shoreditch from the early years of the twentieth century. F. Wrighton & Son had been based in Brampton Road Hackney, but after a spell in Leyton built the Brampton Works in Billet Road in 1933 and was still in business in the late 1960s. Libraco, who made library furniture, including the rapidly vanishing card catalogue cabinets, were based in Walthamstow from 1912 to 1926. There were also important toy makers in the area. A. Wells

142. A.V. Roe on the Lea Marshes, 1909.

and Co was founded around 1920 in Somers Road and as Wells Brimtoy operating from larger premises in Sterling Road, competed successfully with the German toy makers in the inter-war years. The company ceased to trade in 1965. Britains Ltd, once known for toy metal soldiers, built a factory in Sutherland Road in 1951. Britains successfully switched to plastics in 1966 and two years later moved to a larger site on Blackhorse Lane.

PLASTICS

The first plastic in Britain was made in Hackney in 1862. In 1887 the successor business, the British Xylonite Company, moved the production of sheet plastic out to Brantham in Suffolk and in 1896 bought Jack's Farm at Hale End, with the intention of closing down their Homerton operation and moving the remainder of the business to another green-field site. There the company made celluloid and lactoid, a non-inflammable substitute and by 1939 the site was the centre of plastic production for the enlarged Xylonite Group under the brand name 'Halex'. The factory was expanded in 1949, by which time there were 1000 employees, and again in 1960. Today the successor company operates from Brantham but a collection of early plastic objects and trade catalogues survives at Vestry House. The company's trade mark was the elephant and the turtle, while the catalogues from the early twentieth century proclaimed the first mass plastic products 'Cuffs, collars, and fronts' the all-plastic dress accessories.

FILMS

Another early twentieth-century industry alighted briefly in Walthamstow. The first local film studio was built by the Precision Film Company in 1915, while a competitor, the British and Colonial Kinematograph Company took over a roller skating rink on Hoe Street in 1913. Jack Buchanan and Lilian Braithwaite starred in such early classics as *When London Sleeps* in 1914, while the company also made *The Battle of the Somme* in 1916. The studio closed in 1924. For a couple of years from 1913-15 the Cunard Company made films in Wood Street, among its actors was Gladys Cooper. Broadwest Studios took over in 1916, turning to filming books and plays, but went bankrupt in 1924. Two more companies were to use the studios – British Filmcraft even took to the great outdoors for a film series on Dick Turpin, shot in nearby Epping Forest. But competition from the USA and from studios in West London proved too strong and the last film company had gone by 1933.

143. The Xylonite works at Highams Park in 1908.

144. One of the largest firms in Walthamstow was Achille Serre, dyers and dry cleaners, shown here in the 1930s in Blackhorse Lane. By 1961, 1700 people were employed there.

'Fellowship is life': municipality and beyond

146. The coat-of-arms adopted by the new Walthamstow Borough Council. Its motto, 'Fellowship is Life', is borrowed from the writings of a former resident, William Morris.

At the outset of the twentieth century, Walthamstow was in transition. The rapid pace of building had brought in an influx of newcomers, but there were still farms and open spaces in the north of the parish. The cinema had arrived in 1896, and the first local telephone exchange a year later. The decades before the First World War were to see municipal initiatives – council housing, electricity, electric trams, an expanded library service – and the growth of major local industries, including the short-lived film studios. In subsequent years Walthamstow became a borough and matured as part of 'London beyond London', before becoming part of the London Borough of Waltham Forest in 1965.

Aspects of the last hundred years have been covered in earlier chapters, notably on transport, education and work and this last chapter is intended to provide an outline of the other main developments that have affected Walthamstow.

145. A peaceful Walthamstow before the First World War. This is Chapel End c.1905.

As Walthamstow ceased to be a separate local authority in 1965, much of the policy and politics that have affected it belong to a different book on Waltham Forest. However some major developments that have taken place since then, including the growth of the local Asian community, are included.

THE FIRST WORLD WAR

The outbreak of the First World War saw some immediate social changes, large and small. The volunteers for the army included nineteen staff from the UDC trams who had gone by 10 September and the council had to apply for a police licence to employ women conductors. When this was granted in December 1915, Walthamstow became the first authority in the London area to have female employees on its vehicles. Train services were reduced and sporting activity suffered as the Walthamstow Avenue football team – top of the league in the 1902-3 season – ceased to play for the duration. More seriously were anti-German riots. Hackney, with its large German community had seen an outburst in August 1914, and soon afterwards butchers' shops in Wood Street were destroyed. When a German U-boat sunk the passenger ship *Lusitania* in May 1915, there was trouble in Hackney and Walthamstow. Shops with German names in High Street, Hoe Street and St James Street were attacked, with incitement from a local paper.

Zeppelin air raids began in January 1915 and on the night of 17/18 August one crossed Walthamstow. Bombs fell on Lloyd Park, on the Co-operative stores at 189 Hoe Street, and at the junction of Hoe Street and Orford Road. The council asked local shopkeepers to keep their lights to a minimum and street lights were painted green. There was a petition about the flashes of light from the electric trams and as a result drivers were told to return to the depot when there was advance warning of a raid, or stop if searchlights were switched on. In September 1916 Zeppelin SL11 was picked out in local searchlights and eventually shot down over Cuffley. Many pieces ended up in local hands as souvenirs. Walthamstow escaped further air raids until 19/20 May 1918, when a Gotha IV bomber hit Richard's Place, on the east side of Hoe Street. One hundred houses were damaged and six people injured. Although there were no local civilians dead, over 2000 Walthamstow men were killed in action. A local memorial was compiled by library staff and completed in 1921.

POPULATION GROWTH AND HOUSING

By 1932 Walthamstow had become the highest populated non-county borough in England, although the rate of growth had slowed by the 1920s:

1901	96,720
1911	124,580
1921	127,441
1931	132,972

In the immediate aftermath of the First World War, Walthamstow began a move towards incorporation which would give the district borough status. A petition in support was circulated in 1920 and a public enquiry held in the Orford Road town hall in 1921. The outcome was delayed pending the deliberations of Royal Commissions on London Government and there was a further hitch, when the initial petition was deliberately delayed by the Government in 1926. During the General Strike of May of that year, the council had withheld electricity supplies to local factories, thus preventing non-strikers from continuing to work. This had resulted from an ultimatum from the council's employees that unless this action was taken, the electricity workers would strike, in the process shutting down the electric street lighting. But the council was fined for its temporary termination of supply, and the delay was the Government's way of indicating displeasure. Incorporation was finally granted in 1929. The new council took the motto 'Fellowship is Life' from the writings of William Morris, as suggested by the Walthamstow Antiquarian Society. The motto was retained by the London Borough of Waltham Forest for their own coat of arms in 1965.

PARLIAMENTARY REPRESENTATION

Parliamentary representation also altered after the First World War. Before 1918 Walthamstow had formed part of an Essex county division. The MP for the division from 1906-18 was the Liberal Sir John Simon. But in that year it became a parliamentary borough, with two seats, Walthamstow East and West. The boundary between the two ran along the lines of Chingford Road and Hoe Street. Walthamstow West was Labour from 1918-24 and 1929-67. Walthamstow's first mayor, Valentine McEntee (later Baron McEntee) held the seat from 1922-4 and 1929-50. His successor was Clement Attlee, leader of the Labour Party and Prime Minister, who was MP

Talk to your Wife about it.

Most men don't talk to their wives bout what they call "Politics."

Why not?

The women have to spend the men's wages and do their best to make ends meet. They know where the shoe pinches.

During the last few years the prices of nearly all necessities of life have gone up. £1 to-day will only purchase what 17/- would a few years ago.

Your Wife knows this is True.

Your *real* wages have gone down, although you may be getting as much don't find it easy to raise your wages meet the extra cost of living, do you?

Who, then, *is* getting the benefit?

The income of the rich class has goı up to the extent of Two Hundred Mi lions Pounds. Mr. Chiozza Money, tł well known statistician, and others sa so. That is the class which owns tł tools of production—the capital of tł country.

Why can't *you* get some of the iı creased wealth of the country?

Because the whole of the governmer and local administration is run in th interest of property owners. Liberal and Tories, Progressives and Moderate are all managing things for the benef of the rich. "To him that hath sha be given."

So you see

Politics affect the Wife as well as the Husband.

147. A left-wing broadside against Tories, Liberals and Progressives. A Socialist election manifesto in support of Messrs Flute and Sturge, c.1913.

148. The Walthamstow teachers produced this leaflet supporting Messrs Brooks and Woolley and warned of a perceived threat to donations to local charities, c.1914.

The Hamper Fund

AND

The Cripple Fund

are contributed to **not only** by Moderates. but also by Progressives, Teachers and School Children. The Teachers ask you to repudiate all attempts to make political capital out of charity by voting for your old representatives

BROOKS

AND

WOOLLEY

IMPORTANT!

If the charities are made use of politically much support will be withdrawn, and there will be

Less Hampers and Less Outings for Cripples.

from 1950-55. Walthamstow East was Conservative until 1929, from 1931-45 and 1955-66. Walthamstow was reduced to a single seat in the early 1980s, which was held by the Conservatives in the high point of the Thatcher years, but recaptured by Labour in 1992.

1930s DEVELOPMENT

By 1927 only 987 acres of Walthamstow remained undeveloped, most of which lay in the north of the parish. A significant proportion of this was sports ground owned by London companies. The pattern of development was largely completed in the 1930s, with the construction of council housing on Forest Road and at Higham Hill and middle class houses in the north-eastern parts of Walthamstow. At Hale End, which was rapidly assuming its modern name of Highams Park, the shops on the Broadway were built in the early 1930s, Mapperley House was demolished for Mapperley Drive before 1936 and a range of new roads constructed, including Beech Hall Crescent, Evanston Avenue and Warboys Crescent, (all 1930), Richmond Avenue and Oakhill Close (1932), Richmond Crescent and Frinton Drive (1933).

HIGHAM HOUSE AND THE WHITE HOUSE

Parts of the former parkland of Higham House were developed by Warner Estates. After the family seat moved to Brettenham Park in Suffolk, Highams was leased to Lady Somerset and then to the Bishop of St Albans. Eleven acres of the estate were leased out to build the White House in 1905 and this was purchased outright in the following year. The house, designed by Voysey, became the home of the Mallinson family in 1926. Sir Stuart Mallinson lived there until his death in 1981. He had been an area commander of the Home Guard in the Second World War, and created an arboretum in 1953, planted by the famous – appropriately, since the Mallinsons had been timber merchants. Sir Stuart was a close friend of Sir Winston Churchill, who used the White House as his campaign headquarters in the elections of 1950-51 in his seat of Woodford. After the death of Sir Stuart in 1981 there were various proposals for the house, but it was badly damaged by fire in December 1983 and later converted for use by old people.

Higham House was let to Essex County Council in 1919 and became a girls' school. It was sold to the council three years later. The lake and part of the surrounding park had already been acquired by the Corporation of London in 1891; now the remaining ninety acres were laid out for middle class housing from 1930. Montalt Road, on the edge of the new estate, had been built in 1897, and was the site of the promotional office. New roads included Charter Road, Nesta Road (1932) and Tamworth Avenue (1934). Prices for the detached and semi-detached houses ranged from £1000 to £3000.

COUNCIL HOUSING

Both the urban district council, and the borough council that succeeded it in 1929 pursued an active housing policy. The UDC had sent representatives to a conference on housing held at the London County Hall in 1918 and appointed a housing committee in June 1919. The Council made a commitment to build 1,500 houses in the next four years. Much of this took place at Higham Hill and on Hale End Road, where the first group

149. Floods on Hoe Street, a view looking south about 1906. The junction with St Mary's Road is on the left, just beyond Bridge House, with a wine and spirit store and the Irish Shirt and Collar Company. Nearest to the camera is part of the branch of the Stratford Co-op.

of houses was ready by 1920. By 1922, 520 houses had been completed and by 1938 a further 1,100, of which 176 were as a result of slum clearance schemes.

In the immediate period of housing shortages after the Second World War 535 temporary bungalows were built in 1947 on a site near the Highams Park Lake. What was intended as a temporary measure lasted until 1961. The bungalows and roads were cleared in 1963 and the area returned to parkland. Major schemes followed, including 414 flats on Priory Court off Countess Road from 1946, and the redevelopment of parts of the St James area and the Prospect Hill area, where larger Victorian houses were chosen for demolition. In all the Council built 5,151 new dwellings in the borough between 1945 and 1964, and a further 645 on Canvey Island and Billericay in Essex. At the end of its independent existence in 1964-5 Walthamstow Borough Council was demolishing large areas of Victorian terraces in the South Grove and Boundary Road areas for redevelopment.

TOWN HALLS AND ROADS

Until 1941 the council continued to use the Town Hall in Orford Road, with additional offices in Water House in Lloyd Park. In that year the present town hall opened on the site of Chestnuts Farm on Forest Road, next to the South West Essex technical college. The architect was P.D. Hepworth and the original intention was to create a major civic centre. Hepworth's building has a central portico, with a front dominated by a tall square copper-clad clock tower. The Assembly Rooms were added in 1943, but used as a British Restaurant until after the end of the Second World War. The court house to the west dates from 1971-2.

The Ferry Boat bridge was rebuilt in 1915 and ceremoniously opened on 30 March of that year, enabling Forest Road to take more traffic. The first major road scheme of the twentieth century took place in 1927, with the construction of the Lea Valley Viaduct and the first section of the North Circular Road which ran from the Crooked Billet over the marshes and the river to Edmonton. There were fears that it would cut through

150. The old Walthamstow Town Hall in Orford Road.

151. The impressive new Town Hall in Forest Road.

Epping Forest, but the initial route ran parallel to Becontree Avenue to link up with Forest Road. However in 1970 the course of the road was straightened and the largest surviving area of Epping Forest in Walthamstow bisected. However the old road was removed and forest land reinstated. At the same time a covered reservoir was built between Waterworks Corner and the new roundabout on the North Circular Road. A throughway and a bridge over Forest Road linked the two areas of divided forest.

ELECTRICITY

With the worst of the political battles behind it, the urban district council built on the service initiatives of the local board in other areas. An electricity generating station opened in Exeter Road in 1901, which survived in service under the nationalised industry until 1968, being demolished in the following year. In advance of construction 54 miles of cables had been laid along the main streets and 63 electric street lights put up. The new power station also provided current for the UDC's trams and the council was able to offer direct competition with the Lea Bridge District Gas Company for services and household appliances. Electricity showrooms were opened at 212 Hoe Street in 1908, and residents were encouraged to 'hire their wires' at a cheap rate as a way of widening the customer base. The first Hoe Street showrooms were replaced by Electric House on Church Hill, which opened in January 1937. This incorporated offices and workshops for the undertaking. The entrance hall had a lighted fountain and goldfish pond, while the outside was used for garish red, green and yellow electric advertising. The building closed as a regional electricity office in the early 1980s, but is still used for electricity retailing. Walthamstow Borough Council's arms still adorn the pediment.

LIBRARIES, ARCHIVES, MUSEUM AND GALLERY

The library service initiated by the local board was also enlarged. Rosebank, the house taken for the library, was now too small for the expanding service, but the limitations of the penny rate funding capped the level of investment. However an appeal made to the benefactor Andrew Carnegie in February 1908 was successful - Carnegie promised £10,000 for the new building and a new library, including a lecture room, was constructed on the site of Rosebank, which opened in July 1909. The newsroom was retained as an annexe at the rear of the building. The library was damaged in the fire of 1982, but survived, al-

152. Annie Hatley, archaeologist and second curator of Walthamstow Museum. a view taken in the museum office, probably at the time of the re-opening in 1950. At one time a copy hung on the back of the museum door, inscribed in the subject's own hand '...showing the strains of the war years.'

though the lending functions are now housed in a new building on part of the site of the former baths.

Walthamstow's second librarian, George Edward Roebuck, was a significant figure in the library world. In 1919 he suggested that Walthamstow should take the lead in calling a conference of neighbouring local authorities to discuss the limitations of the penny rate, and the effect it had on financing libraries. Roebuck's initiative ultimately led to the abolition of rate limitation. He was also one of the instigators of the creation of the Walthamstow Antiquarian Society in 1915. Roebuck had begun to build up a collection of local historical sources in the library and when a map of the manor of Walthamstow Tony dated 1699 was found rolled up in a drainpipe at the Ferry Boat Inn, it was given to the library. In turn this provided the stimulus to create a local history society to publish the map. George Bosworth provided the notes and the publication was ready for the first meeting of the Society. Roebuck took the opportunity of the abolition of manorial tenure to actively seek the deposit of title deeds and court rolls with the library, and it is due to his actions that Walthamstow owes the core of its historical deposited records.

Roebuck and the WAS were also in partnership to create a local museum. Vestry House had been rented by the Walthamstow Literary and Scientific Institute from 1882, which had provided a reading room and space for a photographic society and a natural history society. The extension, which had been used as an armoury by the local volunteers was taken over by a firm of local builders in 1891 and in the following year the Institute closed. The Charity Governors leased the main building vacated by the Institute to Robert Maynard, who lived there until 1912, when it was taken by Constance Demain-Saunders. The Council had resolved to create a local museum in 1926, and with so many of the older buildings being demolished for redevelopment, there was a growing awareness of the need to save artefacts as well as records. The WAS had tried to save the timbers from Moons Farm barn when that site was taken for housing in 1927, but poor storage led to the ultimate destruction of the preserved material. So when Miss Demain-Saunders offered to surrender the remainder of her lease of Vestry House in 1930, the Council was able to set up a museum, which opened on 2 May 1931.

Records and some local history material were transferred from Central Library to the new museum, which was initially staffed by volunteers from the WAS. A curator was employed from 1933. The lease of the former armoury expired in 1933, and this was added to the museum in 1934. It was fitted out with salvage from two prominent local buildings – panelling and a carved fireplace from Essex Hall, which had been demolished in 1933, and the portico and doorway from Church Hill House, dating from 1784, which also went at the same time.

Vestry House closed in 1939 on the outbreak of war and did not re-open again until 1950. It took in further local history material from Chingford and Leyton in the late 1970s and now serves as the museum and archives and local studies collection for Waltham Forest. Two of the former police cottages were converted to provide the museum with extra storage and office space in 1979-80 and at the time of writing, a major extension is planned, which will provide space to work with school parties. The garden at the rear will be opened to the public, and will include a section recreating what would have been grown for the workhouse inmates.

The re-opening of Vestry House Museum was preceded in October 1950 by the opening of the

William Morris Gallery in Water House by the then Prime Minister, Clement Attlee. The centenary of Morris' birth had been celebrated locally in 1934 and the Gallery now provided a place of display for items associated with Morris, the bequest of paintings of Frank Brangwyn and the Mackmurdo gift of furniture and textiles.

Walthamstow's public library experimented with book delivery to Higham Park from 1896-8 and Higham Hill from 1896-9, but the service was not a success. A branch in a shop opened at Highams Park in 1907, replaced by a purpose-built branch in 1935. Higham Hill got a branch library in 1931. Wood Street library was in the course of construction in September 1939, and was used as a military training workshop and to store cardboard coffins, expected to be needed for massive civilian casualties, which fortunately did not materialise on the scale expected. The library was completed after the end of the war and opened in 1950. Walthamstow's schools' library service was started in 1913.

OPEN SPACES

In 1920 Walthamstow had over forty acres of council maintained parks and there were a further 358 acres of forest, plus thirty acres of Highams Park. There had been an addition to Lloyd Park when twelve acres of the adjoining Aveling Park estate was bought and added and the small Stoneydown gardens opened in 1920.

A major addition came in 1934, when the council obtained legislation to extinguish the remaining grazing rights in the Lammas lands on Walthamstow marshes, effectively ending the conflict between grazing cattle and recreational humans in favour of the latter, although it is likely that the traditional grazing regime had ended twenty years earlier. Claims that had to be settled included compensation for boat hire business and a showman, who used land near the banks for roundabouts, a coconut shy and skittles. Schemes to lay out the land for playing fields, a boating lake, Lido, open air dance platform and ballroom were interrupted by the preparations for war in the late 1930s.

During the war trenches were dug across the Marshes to hamper invading soldiers and filled in in 1949. Subsequently the greatest threat to what was becoming recognised as a significant wild life habitat came in the late 1970s. When the Marshes passed to the Lee Valley Park Authority in 1969, they inherited the permission to extract gravel contained in the Walthamstow Corporation Act of 1956. This danger to the environment of the marshes was not finally averted until 1980 when the Greater London Council refused to provide the necessary planning permission, in part due to the actions of a local pressure group, Save the Marshes. In 1985 the Marshes were designated a Site of Special Scientific Interest, providing added protection.

HOSPITALS

Municipal endeavour also extended to hospitals. A group of local authorities got together to establish a voluntary orthopaedic hospital at Brookfield, Hale End, which functioned from 1923-1939. In 1929 there was a virulent outbreak of smallpox, and the council set up a special hospital at Low Hall farm with forty beds. There were 189 cases before the crisis passed towards the end of 1930. The hospital remained in use until 1940 when it was hit by incendiary bombs. A maternity hospital was opened in Thorpe Combe in Forest Road by the borough in 1934. Chingford Hospital also began as an isolation hospital, opened in the grounds of Larkswood in 1901. It was jointly run with Leyton from 1938. Those services that survived to 1948, including the Connaught Hospital, were all taken over by the National Health Service. The Connaught, which had expanded to include the former town hall from 1958, closed in 1979-80.

THE SECOND WORLD WAR

The Munich crisis of 1938 provided a prelude to war. On 25 September loudspeaker vans toured Walthamstow urging people to be measured up for gas masks, and these were then issued through local school and church halls on 29 September, when 102,000 were distributed. Some 18,000 Anderson shelters were also dug into local back gardens over the next twelve months. In advance of the outbreak of war on 3 September, plans were made to evacuate children, and on 1 September 2,000 mothers and 11,700 children were evacuated by train from Hoe Street and Blackhorse Road stations to Bedfordshire, Hertfordshire, Northamptonshire and Rutland.

Public surface shelters were hastily constructed in advance of the first raids, which began in August 1940, when four bombs fell in the grounds of the White House. The first casualty was on 16 September, when twelve bombs fell on Low Hall farm and the St James Street/Coppermill Lane

153. *The Wrighton furniture making factory was turned over to the manufacture of aeroplane bodies during the last war.*

area. A further 68 people were injured. Parachute mines caused larger blast areas, as at Farnan Avenue. Historic buildings also suffered. St Mary's Church was damaged by incendiaries on the night of 4 October and four days later a high explosive bomb destroyed the older west end of the Monoux Almshouses. Reports of an unexploded bomb beside the church tower turned out to be an exposed lead coffin. Air raids lessened in 1942 and 1943. The last of the piloted raids took place on 19 April, when houses in Highams Park were damaged and two houses in Malvern Avenue completely wrecked. Sixteen people died.

But the worst casualties were caused by the flying bombs, the V1s and the V2 rockets. Fifteen V1s hit Walthamstow between 16 June and the end of August. Several bombs had fallen in the grounds of Low Hall farm, but it was completely destroyed by one of the fifteen. The heaviest casualties were caused by the bomb that fell on Hitchman's distribution centre near the junction of Hoe Street and Church Hill on 16 August 1944. It landed at 10am and many people were queuing at a fish shop on the west side of the road. People took cover in the narrow passageway besides Burton's new shop (opened in 1939) on the north side of the High Street at the Hoe Street junction and were killed as the blast shot up the passage. Twenty-two people died and a further 122 were injured.

The V2s that followed also caused severe damage. One fell on Blackhorse Road in December 1944 damaging 2,700 houses, killing ten people and injuring nearly 100 more. In January 1945 eight people died when a shelter near the junction of Chingford and Nelson roads was hit and in the same month Bawn's factory on Blackhorse Road was hit just after lunch. 17 people died and over 200 injured and the factory was effectively destroyed. In all 299 people died in the wartime bombing, 2,835 were injured and out of the total stock of 32,000 houses, flats and shops, 1,288 were destroyed and a further 28,849 damaged in some way – from broken glass to severe structural damage.

After the war one resident recalled the profusion of wild plants that colonised the ruined and cleared bomb sites – it took several years to rebuild them all.

In the immediate aftermath of the war rationing remained in force, and although lemons, grapefruit and bananas appeared in 1946, many goods were in short supply. The winter of 1946/7 was especially severe, with two months of severe cold, further heavy snow in the first two weeks of March and floods at the end of the second week.

Flood water polluted the Lea Bridge filter beds and for a few days there was no water other than rain water until mobile tanks could get round.

POST-WAR WORLD

There was no census in 1941 but the post-war population showed a drop. In 1951 there were 121,135 people and this fell further by 1961 when there were 108,860. In 1981 the wards of Waltham Forest defined as Walthamstow were home to 64,847 people.

After the war there were many more changes. The last farm was built over in 1950. Salisbury Hall had been used by the Home Guard in the war and was then left empty. Damaged by local youths, it was demolished in 1952, though an archaeological excavation revealed much of its past. Grosvenor House, destroyed in a fire, was demolished. Marsh Street Congregational Church lost its spire in 1954, damaged in the Hoe Street bomb, and Church Hill Methodist Church, badly damaged in the same incident went in the following year. It was not until 1958 that the remains of Burton's shop were replaced by Central Parade on the Church Hill/Hoe Street junction. The former Education offices on the north side of the High Street were cleared in August 1959 in preparation for the construction of the shopping arcade. The Conservative Club building next door followed in 1960, and in the same year the Palace Theatre went.

Major physical developments in the centre of Walthamstow since 1970 have included the demolition of property at the junction of St Mary's Road and Hoe Street as part of the rebuilding of the bus station in the mid 1980s. There have also been alterations north of the High Street including major demolition round the Willow Walk and Palmerston Avenue junction. Houses along Selborne Road were gradually demolished in the late 1970s to make way for new shops, culminating in the Selborne Walk centre, which opened in October 1988.

Appropriately for a multi-cultural community, the opening ceremony included music from the Midnight Blue steel band, Caribbean buskers in full costume, traditional dancing from an African women's group, a limbo dancer, and a clutch of Pearly kings and Queens.

A MULTI-CULTURAL COMMUNITY

Much of Walthamstow's history has been one of incomers, and in the past these included a proportion of people from other lands – Huguenots, whose ancestors had been refugees from persecution in seventeenth-century France, Germans in the mid nineteenth century in search of a better standard of living. In the 1960s and 1970s Walthamstow became home to people from the Caribbean, Africa, and people of Asian origin. In 1981 23% of Walthamstow's population had heads of household born outside the United Kingdom, compared to 21% in Leyton and 5% in Chingford. Although there is a substantial Afro-Caribbean population, the bulk of the ethnic minority people are from the Indian sub-continent, including East Africa.

As in the majority of multi-ethnic communities there have been racial incidents. In 1986 there were 73 reported attacks on people of ethnic minorities, of which 78% were on people of Asian origin. The worst incident to date was an arson attack on the home of Parveen and Yunus Khan in Belgrave Road in July 1981, when petrol was poured through their letter box. Mrs Khan and her three children died in the resulting blaze. Yunus survived but died of a heart attack in 1985, just two months before the police closed the case, having been unable to catch the attackers.

An Asian centre was first proposed for the area in 1981, using the former National School in Orford Road. It was opposed by local Conservatives and there were petitions against the planning application. Approval was obtained in July 1981, but there were financial problems and it was not until 24 November 1983 that the Asian Centre was formally opened by the Prince and Princess of Wales. The Centre is now close to many Asians, who live in the roads to the east and south of

154. The Dar al Uloom Quadria Jilau mosque and religious school, St Mary's Road, 2001

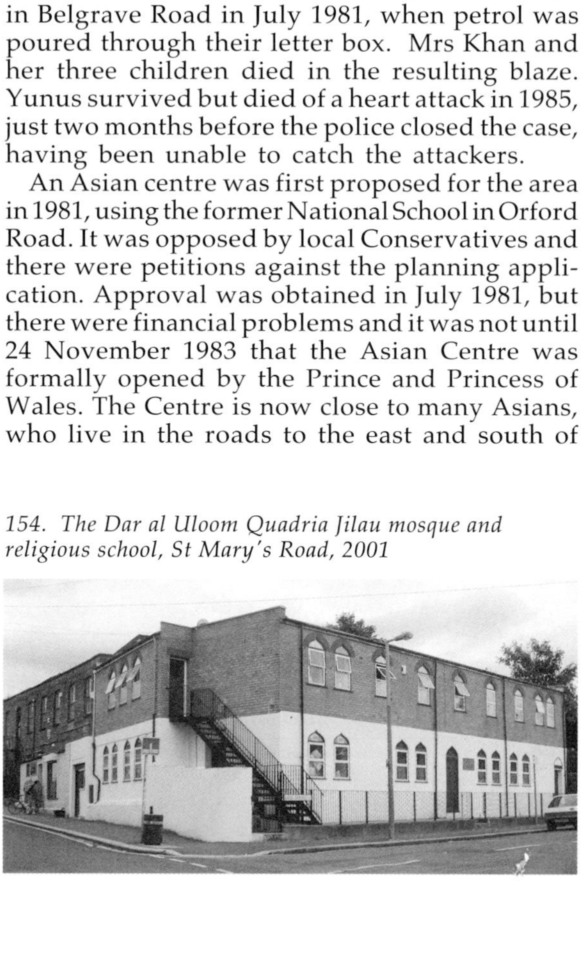

155. Walthamstow market, looking east along the High Street, with the old Central Library building in the background, 2001.

Orford Road. In 1994 other Asian facilities included an Asian Family Resource Centre on Truro Road, the Asian Welfare Society in Second Avenue, and a school to teach Tamil children their mother tongue and provide advice and a social club for older people on Hoe Street. The Ahmadiya Muslim Association for Women on Erskine Road provided sporting activities and religious discussion. A factory on the corner of St Mary Road and East Avenue was converted in the late 1990s to become the Dar al Uloom Quadria Jilania, a mosque and religious school, with a shop alongside selling ornaments, which opened in 2001.

LAST WORDS

There can be no convenient place for a history to call a halt. Since I took my first bus ride to Walthamstow virtually a quarter of a century ago, and walked up Orford Road, past what was then the Connaught Hospital and round the bend with the first glimpse of St Mary's Church ahead and the 1934 restored Ancient House on the right, much has changed – and will continue to do so. The construction of the Victoria Line in 1968 has made it easy for commuters to get into central London, and house prices have encouraged many more incomers to look at Walthamstow and what it can offer – the Forest, a lively High Street market, a diverse range of communities. Estate agents have been at work to invent new place names and some, like Walthamstow Village, have stuck, though many would be hard put to define where the 'village' ends and the rest of central Walthamstow begins. Despite the losses, a range of historic houses survive, and some of the earlier cottage homes, like Ebenezer Clarke's Eden Grove development. There are many more echoes of the past – the curves in the Shernhall Street following the course of the lost stream and lost field boundaries, as well as physical reminders of the gentlemen's landscape in Highams Park. I hope that this book will prompt some to discover more.

Sources

Between the wood and the water

The bulk of this chapter is based on the Coe Map of Walthamstow of 1822, *John Coe's Map of Walthamstow in 1822* (WAS, 1966, with notes by A.D.Law); the *Victoria County History of Essex* Vol VI, Walthamstow. *Vestiges* Nos 86-88 and the photocopies of the Walthamstow Vestry minutes up to 1820. I have also used P.H.Reaney's *Place Names of Essex* pp 104-6.

No vestry minutes for the parish period of government survive after 1820 and the account of the acceptance of the Coe map is an imaginative reconstruction.

The log boat reference comes from *Strength in the Tower, an illustrated history of Hackney* by David Mander (Sutton Publishing, 1998), p4. The Roman pot is mentioned in *The Forest in Walthamstow and Chingford* by A.D.Law and Septimus Barry (WAS/CHS, 1978) p 15. Game's ferry is recalled in *Across the years, Walthamstow Memories* edited by Annie R. Hatley (WAS, 1953)

Manors

VCH Vol VI (ibid), *Vestiges,* Nos 86-90, 111-114. *The Forest in Walthamstow and Chingford* (ibid) pp5-8)

House and hamlet

Vestiges Nos 97-99, 102, 105, 106, 111, 114, 122-123, *VCH* Vol VI, James M.Gibson, *The Walthamstow Charities, Caring for the Poor 1500-2000* (Phillimore, 2000). A.D.Law, *Walthamstow Village, an account of Church End.* (5th rev. ed. WHS, 1996); Philip C. Plummer and Walter H. Bowyer, *A brief history of Courtenay Warner and Warner Estate* (WAS, 2000); Coe map of Walthamstow, 1822; Ordnance Survey 25" to 1 mile sheets for the 1870 and 1912-14 editions. Additional details from a lecture given by Gary Butler to the Walthamstow Amenity Society on 6 February 2001. George Gascoigne's biography has been supplemented by the article by John Butler at www.luminarium.org/renlit/gascbio

Places to pray

VCH ibid; Vestiges 89-90, 97-9. Gibson *op cit. Guide to St Mary's Church* (nd) *Nonconformity in Walthamstow,* Vols 1 & 2 M.E.Batsford (WAS 1977, 1979)

Parochial People 1660-1860

VHM W 96 COL for the Collards (My introduction to the list and esp 2/2/2 for George Collard's accounts, 2/2/8 for Mrs Smith and unlisted papers for the divorce settlement (dated 1863) and the case of the decanters; Jane Bredell's inventory is W96 COL 4/3; *Some more Walthamstow Houses,* George F. Bosworth (WAS, 1933); *Biographical notes relating to certain members of the Wigram family,* Reginald S. Wigram (Author, 1912); *Some Walthamstow houses,* George F. Bosworth (WAS, 1924); *Some more Walthamstow Houses,* George F. Bosworth (WAS 1933), though there is some confusion for William Houghton's dates; Census returns for Walthamstow 1871 for the Houghtons and Benjamin Warwick; the additional description of dark houses is from *Across the Years, Walthamstow memories* (WAS, 1953); Vestiges Nos 103; VHM Acc 10185 *Joel Johnson's memoirs,* from the copy owned by Mrs Evan Edwards of Denmark Hill in 1829; Vestiges No 102; VHM W 72.2 Highams for Humphry Repton's Red Book of Highams, quoted by kind permission of Sir Henry Warner, Bart; *Epping Forest then and now,* Winston G.Ramsey with Reginald L. Fowkes (Battle of Britain Prints International Ltd, 1986)

Governing the parish

VCH Vol VI ibid. Vestiges Nos 97-99; VHM DA400/A2/14/2 *Inquisition held at Stratford Langthorne... charged with the reformation of decipt and breaches of trust of the Monoux Charity, 4 August 1636;* Gibson *op cit.* VHM W47.1 Z1 (perambulations)

Let him not eat: the problem of the poor

Gibson *op cit;* Vestiges No 102; *VCH* Vol VI ibid. *The history of Vestry House from workhouse to museum,* Vestry House Museum (unpublished text, 1998); VHM W 34.41 E12 apprentice register 1808-19; W34.41 A7 Overseers accounts; W 34.5 M5 Overseer's day book 1834-6; W34.41 M 1 Workhouse minutes 1834-5

Laying Down the Law

VCH ibid. *A William Holcroft his booke, local office-holding in late Stuart Essex.* J.A. Sharpe, editor (Essex Record Office, 1986); Vestiges 91, 102-104; *Across the years. Walthamstow Memories* Edited by Annie R.Hatley (1953); *The history of Vestry House* ... ibid

Transport
VCH Vol VI articles on Leyton and Walthamstow. *The Lea Bridge Turnpike and the Wragg Stage Coaches.* W.G.S. Tonkin (WAS 1974); *The Tramways of East London*, Rodinglea (Tramway & Light Railway Soc. 1967); *A history of the development of Walthamstow*, Richard Wall. (M. Phil thesis, 1968); *The Walthamstow and Chingford Railway* C.C. Pond (WAS, 1982)

Vigorous Victorians: developing a suburb
VCH ibid, esp p 243-5, 280-2, 294-302; *A history of the development of Walthamstow.* Richard Wall (unpublished M. Phil thesis, 1968); Vestiges Nos 100, 103, 104; *Our local press: a short historical account of the newspapers in Walthamstow*, R.G. Desmond (WAS, 1955). *A brief history of Courtenay Warner & Warner estate.* Philip C. Plumer and Walter H.Bowyer (WHS, 2000); E.W's letter from the *Walthamstow Guardian* as cited in text. Plans from Clarke Orme collection at VHM, copied from aperture cards M961-2, M1113, M1164 and M1164i. Mrs Eason's amendments were not accessible at the time of conducting the research; VHM W34.9 for the burial board, esp W8.5 for Robinson's letter and W 4.3 Morgan's apology; I was unable to trace the source for the exploding manhole cover again, but believe it was a *Walthamstow Guardian* report, seen in the late 1970s; *Walthamstow water supply*, Alice and Peter Hogg, George and Violet Rhodes (WAS 1986); *Nonconformity in Walthamstow Vols 1-2 op cit. The Walthamstow Charities ... op cit.* The Bird election card was also not traced at the time of writing but existed in the VHM political ephemera collections.

Learning for Life
VCH ibid; Vestiges no 103; *Walthamstow Village* (5th rev ed, WAS 1996); *Forest School 1834-1984* (The School, 1984). *The history of Vestry House ...* ibid; *George Monoux's School, Walthamstow 1527-1977*, C.C. Pond (WAS, 1977); Gibson, *op cit*; obituary of Ian Dury in *The Independent*, 28 March 2000 and lyrics of *New Boots and Panties* (Stiff Records, 1977).

Shops and shows
VCH ibid. Vestiges 104,108-109, 122-123; *Shopper's Paradise, a history of High Street, Walthamstow* J.W. Howes and A.D. Law (WHS, 1991); *Clarkes History of Walthamstow* Ebenezer Clarke (original Joseph Shillinglaw 1861, reprinted with new introduction by WAS, 1980); *Victorian and Edwardian Waltham Forest* compiled by W.G.S. Tonkin (WAS 1973); *Right up your street: a short history of Wood Street*, J.W. Howes and A.D. Law (WHS, 1994); personal knowledge of background of saving of Jones' shop; W 96 SOL 1-4 for Elizabeth Solly's letters; W96 COL uncatalogued for the Kemble hand bill; *A history of the development of Walthamstow*, Richard Wall (unpublished M. Phil thesis, 1968) – including John Hitchman's social night; *Seventy years a club: being a brief record of the formation of and events in the life of the Walthamstow Working Men's Club and Institute ... 1862-1912*, Ambrose Barker (2nd ed rev to 1932); *From parochial to popular: the development of entertainment in a London suburb, Walthamstow 1860-1920*, Anita Miller (unpublished dissertation, 1995); *Our local press: a short historical account of the newspapers in Walthamstow*, R.G. Desmond (WAS, 1955).

Working World
VCH op. cite. *Across the years op cit; Walthamstow marsh: a guide to the history of the area* (Lee Valley Park Authority, 1986). *The Walthamstow Windmill and Essex Windmills today* A.D. Law and W.G.S. Tonkin (WAS 1970, rp 1996). The A.V. Roe quote is from *The World of Wings and things*, the autobiography of Sir Alliot Verdon Roe, (Hurst and Blackett, 1939) quoted in *Walthamstow marsh...; Strength in the tower: an illustrated history of Hackney*, David Mander (Sutton Publishing, 1998) for BXL.

'Fellowship is life'
VCH ibid; Vestiges Nos 105-106, 117,123; *Late Extra, Hackney in the News* David Mander (Sutton Publishing, 2000) for the Hackney anti-German riots; *Brief history of Warner estate ibid; The Forest in Walthamstow and Chingford* by A.D. Law and Septimus Barry (WAS/CHS, 1978) for the temporary bungalows; *Walthamstow marshes and lammas rights*, G.A.Blakeley (WAS, 1951); *Walthamstow Marsh: a guide to the history of the area* (Lee Valley Park Authority, 1986); *The war over Walthamstow*, Ross Wyld (Walthamstow B.C., 1945 reprinted LBWF, 1989) VHM subject files on the Asian Centre and Selborne Walk shopping centre; *Racial attacks and harassment 1987*, LB Waltham Forest Race Relations Unit; statistics on population from LB Waltham Forest data 1985 and 1991 and from 1981 census data; *Beneath the surface: an inquiry into racial harassment in LB Waltham Forest 1988-90. Asian Community Information Guidelines* (LB Waltham Forest, 1994).

Index

Asterisks denote illustrations or captions.